# ATTACK

## OF THE HMS

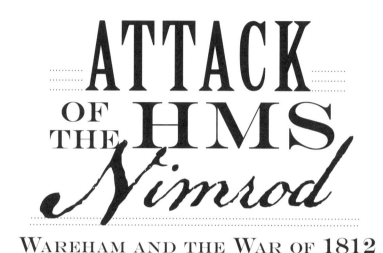

### WAREHAM AND THE WAR OF 1812

# J. NORTH CONWAY & JESSE DUBUC

Charleston · London

THE
History
PRESS

Published by The History Press
Charleston, SC 29403
www.historypress.net

Copyright © 2014 by J. North Conway and Jesse Dubuc
All rights reserved

First published 2014

Manufactured in the United States

ISBN 978.1.62619.409.0

Library of Congress CIP data applied for.

*For my mother, my most stubborn fan and supporter.*
*—Jesse Dubuc*

# CONTENTS

# ACKNOWLEDGEMENTS

*Thanks to the following:*

WAREHAM SUMMER OF CELEBRATION COMMITTEE:
Coordinator: Claire Smith
President: Rudy Santos
Vice-president: Nancy Miller
Clerk: Angela Dunham
Treasurer: Robert Powilatis
Board of directors: Sharon Boyer, Jovina Dean, Eleanor Martin, Malcolm Phinney, W. Robert White
Committee members: Nora Bicki, Robert Blair, Linda Burke, Mary Jane Burke, Jacqui Healey, William Heaney, Mel Lazarus, Laura Lopes, Deborah McGonnell, John McGonnell, Clifford Sylvia, Paula Tufts

LIBRARY BOARD OF TRUSTEES:
Chair: Bethany Gay
Vice-chair: Roger Bacchieri
Secretary: William White
Members: Johnna Fredrickson, Rachel Kuklinski, M. Kathleen LaFlamme Diane O'Brien
Liaison to the board: Judy Whiteside

WAREHAM HISTORICAL COMMISSION:
Chair: Angela M. Dunham
Vice-chair: Mack Phinney
Treasurer: Len Boutin
Clerk: Cheryl Knapp
Board of selectmen liaison: Alan Slavin

WAREHAM HISTORICAL SOCIETY OFFICERS:
President: Angela M. Dunham
Vice-president: Mary Hull
Treasurer: Sandy Slavin
Secretary: Cathy Phinney

WAREHAM HISTORICAL SOCIETY BOARD MEMBERS:
June Strunk
Joella Cruz
Bernard Greenwood
Paul Girard
Alan Slavin
David Warr

AUTHORS:
Scott Ridley
Michael Tougias
Will Staples
Jennifer Reeser

PUBLISHING:
Tris Coburn, literary agent
Dani McGrath, Northeast sales, The History Press
Tabitha Dulla, commissioning editor, The History Press
Darcy Mahan, project editor, The History Press

# IN CROSSING

*Commemorative Poem by Katy Whittingham*

## 1814–2014

> *As far from time—as History*
> *As near yourself—as Today*
> *—Emily Dickinson*

Over the highest spar, can you picture a community?
Sketch and shade with predetermined destiny
and neatly settled susceptibility?
In its age of arranged marriage between land and water,
orphaned islands, crooked rivers,
high harvests: cotton, rods, nails, bread,
can you still hear the tall sea tale
as it once washed over the weary waterman
in decidedly neutral beds?
Stop, and listen to the expectant hum
before orders, before eighteen guns, before
a simple sound could sunder, and not so simple men
might propose a peaceful end—
There are not always words that can capture, but when
they do they can be too powerfully accurate,
as brazen and blazing as that infamous red glare,
urgent as surge winds and heavily burdened like iron rails—
what choice did twelve Fearing men have

but to stand for all of the others, among them,
Cape cousins: Fancy, Nancy, and Elizabeth.
Yet, chance is chance, and fortitude
matches with what sea souls might expect.
As an elephant will run from a bee,
the mightier many set off on their watercourse
with deserted vow to come back.
But with waters crossed, history did change,
once marched streets now call out names,
and the earlier picture—a little tired in form,
yet finely grained with preserved intent,
may be mounted in the celebratory frame,
in honor of the value secured,
positioned at the arch of our inviting gateway.

*Wareham resident* KATY WHITTINGHAM *is a poet and educator. Her book of poems,* By a Different Ocean, *was published by Plan B Press in Virginia in 2009. She teaches English at the University of Massachusetts–Dartmouth and Bridgewater State University.*

# *Introduction*

# THE YIN AND YANG
# OF HISTORY

*History is important. If you don't know history it is as if you were born yesterday.*
*—Howard Zinn*

Fiction is easy. Nonfiction is hard. Writing nonfiction, you only have so much to work with, and you still have to make it entertaining and enlightening for the reader. With fiction you can make stuff up—vampires attack, there's a car chase, it was all a dream. You don't have that latitude with nonfiction. It is what it is. You only know what you know. It's not like you can write a different ending to a particular historic event—and then John Wilkes Booth was tackled by the brave Secret Service agent who saved President Lincoln's life at the Ford Theater that night.

This is a true story. There is no fiction involved. There is no Hollywood ending to this story. Sorry. But despite it being nonfiction, it is still an important story. That's what writers do: they tell stories. Jesse Dubuc, my coauthor, is a historian. Historians make sure the facts are correct. So with this book, you get the best of both worlds: a story and correct facts.

# A PLEASURE TO WRITE

It is with the greatest pleasure that I accepted the opportunity to write this book about the attack on Wareham in June 1814 by the British navy vessel the HMS *Nimrod*. I am also exponentially pleased that Jesse Dubuc, an extraordinarily talented local historian and Bridgewater State University graduate, agreed to join me in writing it. And further, I am genuinely exultant that Wareham poet and university professor Katy Whittingham agreed to write a commemorative poem for the book. If that all isn't great, I don't know what is.

# ONE BOOK AFTER ANOTHER

This is my twelfth nonfiction book. It is also the sixth book I have written in six years, beginning in 2008 with the publication of another one of my books with The History Press, *The Cape Cod Canal: Breaking Through the Bared and Bended Arm*. This book was followed by a trilogy on New York City during the Gilded Age that included *King of Heists* (2009), *The Big Policeman* (2010) and *Bag of Bones* (2011), all published by Globe Pequot/Lyons Press. In 2012, I wrote a fourth book on New York City called *Queen of Thieves*, scheduled for publication in the fall of 2014 by Sky Horse Publishing. In the summer of 2013, I was contracted by Cadent Press in Maine to coauthor, with Michael Vieira, an illustrated coffee-table book, *The Weather Outside Is Frightful*, a compendium of the worst hurricanes, snowstorms, floods and other natural disasters in New England. The book is due out in October 2014. Busy, busy.

In August 2013, The History Press contacted me about writing two books, one on the history of Wareham and another on the warship *Nimrod*. These two books were to coincide with the 275th anniversary of the town's incorporation and the 200th anniversary of the attack of the British warship *Nimrod* on Wareham in 1814 during the war of 1812. Since I was unable to write both books due to other publishing commitments, I suggested that Michael Vieira write the Wareham book and that I would write the *Nimrod* book. The History Press agreed.

I am also the author of *Shipwrecks of New England* (2000), *New England Visionaries* (1998) and *New England Women of Substance* (1996), all published by Douglas Charles Press; *American Literacy: Fifty Books That Define Our Culture and Ourselves*, published by William Morrow in 1994; and *From*

*Coup to Nuts: A Revolutionary Cookbook*, published in 1987 by Quinlan Press. Good for me.

This is what we call in the publishing business "a plug." My agent, Tris Coburn, in Maine, says my career won't be worth a plugged nickel if I don't do such things. I trust Tris. If it weren't for him, I would not have sold as many books as I have. He has sold everything I have ever written.

## BECOMING A WRITER

Like Katy Whittingham, I also teach at several universities and colleges. I teach writing at Bristol Community College in Fall River, the University of Massachusetts in Dartmouth and Bridgewater State University in Bridgewater, Massachusetts. I tell all my students that there are two types of teachers they will run into in college and university. They are teachers who write and writers who teach. I am of the latter grouping. I write and teach. I also tell my students that neither a teacher who writes nor a writer who teaches is any better or worse than the other. I tell them that each brings a different perspective to the writing process. Teachers who write often bring a theoretical point of view to the process. Writers who teach often focus on practical application. I often ask my students how many of them want to be writers. Often many hands go up. I tell them this: "Why would you want to go looking for rejection when there is already so much of it in your life already?" Practical.

If that doesn't work to dissuade them, I tell them this: "If you write, you will get rejected a lot, but nobody cares how many times you get knocked down. They only care how many times you get back up." More practicality.

Finally, I tell them that when they ultimately do sell a book and then begin to complain about how little money they got and how difficult the writing business is, that they should ask themselves the following question: "Who asked you to be a writer anyway?" Can't get more practical than that.

## ALL MY FRIENDS ARE WRITERS

I do not encourage people to become writers. It is a lonely profession. You don't have many friends, and most of the friends you do end up having are usually writers like yourself. Almost all my friends are writers. I contacted many of them as I began writing this book about the attack on Wareham by the *Nimrod*, seeking their advice or asking them to provide some insight into the historic event. One of the first people I contacted was Scott Ridley in East Harwich, Massachusetts, way down deep in the heart of Cape Cod. Scott is the author of several acclaimed books, most notably and recently *Morning of Fire: John Kendrick's Daring American Odyssey in the Pacific*. Kendrick lived in Wareham, and his home there is now a museum. Kendrick is famous for becoming the first American to sail into the closed nation of Japan in 1791. Scott is also the coauthor, with Richard Rudolph, of the book *Power Struggle: The Hundred-Year War Over Electricity*. Scott and I go way back: we went to the University of Massachusetts in Amherst in 1968, and he was the best man at my wedding in 1971. Last year, his book *Morning of Fire* and my book *Bag of Bones* were published and released two days apart. Small world.

My other writer friends include Michael Tougias, the author of a slew of books about men against the sea, including *Overboard, Ten Hours Until Dawn, The Finest Hours* and *Fatal Forecast*, which is being made into a movie by Disney Studios. Mike and I met more than twenty years ago when he was working on a small book about the history of the Taunton River. At the time, I was working as a writer for the *Providence Journal* and had written a two-part feature on the history of the river. (The Taunton River empties into Mount Hope Bay along the Massachusetts and Rhode Island border.) I was also living in a great old house located just along the banks of the river. One sunny summer afternoon when I was sitting out on my front porch that faced the river, Mike came paddling downriver in his canoe and came ashore in front of my place. He came up onto the porch, introduced himself and explained that he was a writer working on a book about the Taunton River, and we have been friends ever since. Subsequently, Mike and I became writers for the same publisher, Covered Bridge Press. I contacted Mike about writing this book to pick his brain. Mike seldom contacts me to pick my brain. Slim pickings here, I guess.

My other writer friend is the Hollywood scriptwriter Will Staples. Will is working on scripts for Ben Affleck and James Cameron. He's pretty hot stuff. He is also the scriptwriter for the film version of one of my books, *King of Heists*, which was sold to Black Bear Pictures and Jeremy Renner. They still haven't made it into a movie, but they bought the option. Time will tell. I spoke with Will briefly before beginning this book.

My writer friends also include a number of poets. Obviously, Katy Whittingham is one of them. Jennifer Reeser, from Louisiana, is another.

She is the author of several books of poetry, including *An Alabaster Flask*, *Winterproof* and *Sonnets from the Dark Lady and Other Poems*. Jennifer and I have been friends for a long time. Back in July 2005, my poem "The Agamemnon Rag" was published in *Poetry*. This publication, founded by Harriet Monroe in 1912, is considered the Holy Grail for poets. Jennifer contacted me to congratulate me. I told her not to worry, that she would soon be published by *Poetry* as well because her poems were so good. My poem "The Agamemnon Rag" was not necessarily "good" as much as it was funny—and nobody likes funny when it comes to poetry. Sure enough, in December 2005, Jennifer's poem "Blue-Crested Cry" was published in *Poetry*. Good for her. There was absolutely nothing funny about her poem.

So prior to beginning work on this book, I consulted with my few writer friends, and I remain thankful for their kind and generous advice.

# The War of 1812

I did not know about the attack on Wareham by the *Nimrod* until I was contracted to write the book. I am, however, very familiar with the town of Wareham. When my boys, Nate and Andrew, were younger, I used to take them to Onset Beach in Wareham, and we used to stroll along the Onset promenade overlooking the beach where we would buy ice cream, soda and other treats.

My son Nate subsequently moved to Wareham and my granddaughters, Aria and Ella, now live there. I go to the scallop festival and cranberry festival every year in Wareham, and an old friend of mine, Bucky Manning, used to own a bicycle shop near there in Bourne. Still, I was not familiar with the *Nimrod* attack until I began writing this book.

The story of the *Nimrod* attack is plenty exciting, especially against the backdrop of the War of 1812, a war that most Americans did not want and one that neither side won. The British fleet blockaded many New England ports and attacked a number of towns, including Hampden, Maine; Stonington, Connecticut; and Wareham, Massachusetts, among many others. The War of 1812 is often referred as the "Second War of Independence" by some American historians. It was a thirty-two-month military conflict between the United States on one side and Great Britain, its colonies and its Indian allies in North America on the other. It was the United States that declared war. On June 1, 1812, President James Madison sent a message to Congress outlining a list of grievances against the British, among them trade restrictions enforced by Britain because of its continuing war with France, the seizure of American merchant ships, the impressment of American sailors into the Royal Navy and British support of American Indian tribes against American expansion in the north (Canada).

Although President Madison did not specifically ask for a declaration of war, the United States House of Representatives deliberated for four days before voting in favor of the new nation's first declaration of war. The war officially began on June 18, 1812, and it was fought in three major locales throughout the country. At sea, British and American warships and privateers attacked each other's merchant ships. The British, who had a larger, more sophisticated navy, blockaded ports along the Atlantic coast of the United States, including Cape Cod. They carried out landing party raids along the coast, most notably the burning of the capital, Washington, D.C., then known as Washington City, on August 24, 1814.

Many history scholars maintain that the war was a British victory and that the Americans were defeated. They maintain that the British achieved their military objectives by ending America's invasion of Canada and that Canada retained its independence of the United States. They also hold that America lost its bid to stop British impressment of American sailors. This did not happen until the end of the Napoleonic Wars in 1815. The War of 1812 ended with the signing of the Treaty of Ghent in December 1814. The terms called for all Canadian territory previously occupied by American forces to be returned and the pre–War of 1812 boundary between Canada and the United States restored.

# Heroes Galore

There are any number of Wareham heroes in this story, including Ebenezer Bourne, who alerted the town of the pending attack with his cries of "The British are coming! The British are coming!" There is Captain Israel Fearing Jr., the eldest militia officer in town during the British attack, who rallied a small band of Wareham men and tried to intercept the invading troops. There is Dr. Andrew Mackie, the town physician, who was held hostage by the British forces as they made their escape. And there are the other nameless men and women who put out the cotton factory fire that was started by the British forces and worked to rebuild the town after the attack. But there is no Hollywood ending to this story. The damage done in Wareham was more than $20,000, comparable to nearly $1 million by today's estimates. A total of four schooners, five sloops, a ship, a brig and a ship being built at William Fearing's shipyard were set afire. Houses were burned and supplies ransacked. The British left unscathed.

# THE YIN AND YANG OF WAR

Like in any war, the War of 1812 had its yin and yang: two opposing forces, governing the universe, where one force dominates and then is replaced by the other force so that no one force can dominate permanently. The yin: the British burned Washington, D.C., on August 24, 1814, setting fire to many public buildings, including the White House and the Capitol. The yang: we got the "The Star-Spangled Banner," the national anthem of the United States written in 1814 by Francis Scott Key.

The yin: the British burned and looted Hampden, Maine, in September 1814. The yang: the attack propelled the movement for the independence of Maine, which was then part of Massachusetts. Maine achieved statehood in 1820.

The yin: the HMS *Nimrod* attacked Wareham, Massachusetts, on June 13, 1814, burning houses, businesses and ships and holding several Wareham residents hostage. The yang: Wareham today is a prosperous, thriving town with a population of around twenty-two thousand with flourishing tourism, a diversified industrial and commercial economy and an abundance of natural resources, including fifty-four miles of striking beaches, rivers and ponds. It is said that the best revenge is to live well. Surely Wareham is a living example of this age-old adage.

On behalf of Jesse Dubuc, Katy Whittingham and myself, thank you for your attention, and we hope you enjoy this true-life story about the attack of the HMS *Nimrod* on the town of Wareham.

—J. North Conway

# Chapter 1
# THE BRITISH ARE COMING

*And so through the night went his cry of alarm…*
*—Henry Wadsworth Longfellow*

The British are coming! The British are coming!" Ebenezer Bourne cried throughout the sleepy town of Wareham, Massachusetts, on June 13, 1814.

This, of course, wasn't the first time these prophetic words were purportedly used as a rallying cry for New England patriots. Paul Revere is best known for expounding these iconic words on April 18, 1775, when he reportedly made his historic ride through the night through every Massachusetts Middlesex County town, warning of a pending attack by British troops and to alert John Hancock, Samuel Adams and other Patriots that the British were approaching Lexington that evening. The British troops were on the move, beginning a march from Boston to Lexington, presumably to arrest Hancock and Adams and seize the rebel weapon stores hidden in Concord.

Revere's ride and his historic words were memorialized in Henry Wadsworth Longfellow's famous 1861 poem, "The Midnight Ride of Paul Revere," which states, "And so through the night went his cry of alarm / To every Middlesex village and farm,—"

Ebenezer Bourne's gravestone in Wareham. Bourne alerted the selectmen of the town with a fitful cry of "The British are coming! The British are coming!" when he spied a squadron of British ships off the Mattapoisett coast on June 13, 1814. *Courtesy of Andrew Griffith.*

Ironically, Longfellow never mentions the famous rallying cry "The British are coming" in his poem, and from a purely historical perspective, Longfellow got it all wrong. Revere did spread the word of the pending British attack on Concord and Lexington, but there were several riders that night. Two other men, William Dawes and Samuel Prescott, rode with him to spread the word. Reportedly, as many as forty different men on horseback were spreading the word across Boston's Middlesex County.

Another misconception perpetuated by Longfellow's poem was that Revere reached Concord, which he never did. When the three riders were almost overtaken by British troops, they split up, heading in different directions. Historically speaking, Revere was apprehended by the British at Lexington, Dawes fell off his horse and only Prescott was able to warn Concord's residents.

Also, since alerting the countryside was supposed to be done as discreetly as possible, everything depended on secrecy. Middlesex County was crawling British troops, and so the likelihood that Revere yelled anything is doubtful. Besides, at the time, 1775, there had been no revolution, so colonists considered themselves British subjects. According to eyewitness reporting and based on Paul Revere's own account, what he conveyed to households during his ride was simply, "The Regulars are coming out."

# THE BEGINNINGS OF THE WAR OF 1812

Based on most firsthand reports, Wareham's Ebenezer Bourne did, in fact, alert the selectmen of the town with a fitful cry of, "The British are coming! The British are coming!" when he spied a squadron of British ships off the Mattapoisett coast.

Mattapoisett is a southwestern town in Plymouth County. Buzzards Bay lies to the south and the town of Wareham to the north, after the town of Marion. The word "Mattapoisett" is Wampanoag Indian for "a place of resting." The British warship HMS *Nimrod*, considered to be one of the most dreaded British ships, had been patrolling the waters of Buzzards Bay in June 1814.

The country was in the midst of its second war with Britain, the War of 1812. The war was often referred to by historians as the "Second War of Independence." Although President Madison did not specifically ask for a declaration of war, the United States House of Representatives deliberated for four days before voting seventy-nine to forty-nine in favor of the new nation's first declaration of war. The U.S. Senate followed suit. The war officially began on June 18, 1812, when Madison signed the measure into law and proclaimed it the next day.

Following the defeat of the American forces at the Battle of Bladensburg, a British force led by British major general Robert Ross occupied Washington City and set fire to many public buildings. The facilities of the U.S. government, including the White House and U.S. Capitol, were largely destroyed. This was the only time since the Revolutionary War that a foreign power captured and occupied the United States capital.

The second war front included both land and naval battles fought on the American and Canadian border, which ran along the Great Lakes, the Saint Lawrence River and the northern most point of Lake Champlain.

The third battleground was in the South and along the Gulf Coast, where American forces defeated a British invasion force at New Orleans.

# WAREHAM UNPREPARED

According to James Ellis in his book *A Ruinous and Unhappy War: New England and the War of 1812*, "Ebenezer Bourne earlier noticed the path of the ship [HMS *Nimrod*], recognized the danger, and raced to Wareham to spread the alarm."

There were, in fact, two British warships off the Wareham coast: the HMS *Nimrod*, considered the scourge of the New England coast, and the HMS *Superb*. According to Ellis, Wareham had hoped "the war would pass it by," but unlike many of its neighboring communities, like the Cape Cod town of Falmouth, Wareham did not take any extraordinary steps to protect itself from a British assault. Massachusetts state law at the time mandated that towns like Wareham maintain militia companies, but Wareham only met the minimum requirements of this duty. The town fathers had portrayed the town as neutral in the ongoing War of 1812 and accordingly derived a certain sense of false security that it would not face the wrath of any British endeavors. According to town records, the inhabitants of Wareham at the time spent more time securing its shellfish beds than they did fortifying the town from attack by the British. This lack of preparation ultimately proved costly to the town.

## THE BATTLE OF FALMOUTH

Falmouth lies on the southwestern tip of Cape Cod with Vineyard Sound to the south and Buzzards Bay located to the west. The nearby town of Falmouth experienced short-lived but costly damage in the War of 1812 from the HMS *Nimrod*. The area around Falmouth Heights along its southernmost coast was bombarded by several British frigates, including the *Nimrod*, but the Falmouth militia quickly embedded itself on the dunes along the coast and repelled a possible British invasion. The HMS *Nimrod* and other British warships patrolled the New England coast in an effort to limit American shipping during the war.

The town of Falmouth was under continued attack by the British. Its strategic location allowed the militia to fire on British ships passing along the Cape's southernmost shoreline. The Falmouth Artillery Company, a ragtag militia at most, and their small cannons were, according to Jack Sheedy's book *Cape Cod Companion: The History and Mystery of Old Cape Cod*, "little more than an irritant to the British." The HMS *Nimrod* was sent to end the attacks by the Falmouth militia.

On January 28, 1814, the ship anchored off the coast of Falmouth, raised a flag of truce and sent a boat ashore. The commander of the *Nimrod* sent a message demanding that the inhabitants surrender their cannons or risk bombardment. According to local legend, Falmouth's militia captain Weston Jenkins responded, "If you want our cannon, you can come and get them, and we will give you what's in them first." Falmouth refused to give up its arsenal of armaments, and the British retaliated by firing on the town. The commander of the *Nimrod* gave Falmouth inhabitants two hours to seek refuge for women, children and the sick, elderly and infirmed. The townsfolk sought cover while neighboring militia streamed into the town to fortify defenses. The bombardment of Falmouth began at noon and continued into the night. Although the *Nimrod* forces made an attempt at a landing, it was futile, and on second thought, the commander of the *Nimrod* decided against an invasion given the strength of the Falmouth militia that was positioned all along the coast, hunkered down across the grassy dunes. The next morning on January 29, the *Nimrod* set sail for Rhode Island, firing a few warning shots as it passed Nobsque Point. No casualties or injuries were inflicted by the bombardment, but considerable damage was done to homes, buildings and the town's salt works. The results of the cannon bombardment are still visible in some places in Falmouth today. According to newspaper accounts, there is a cannonball hole visible to patrons of a Falmouth a restaurant aptly called the Nimrod. A cannonball hole can be found in the men's room.

## CROCKER'S LETTER

Captain John Crocker of Falmouth penned a scathing letter to the *New England Palladium*, a Boston newspaper, the day after the attack. In it, he described the horrific attack on the town.

"I desire you to notice in your paper that yesterday morning the Nimrod Brig… anchored near this town…and demanded the two field-pieces, and a sloop lying at the wharf…in case of non-compliance threatened to bombard the town. Their demand being refused, the captain then gave notice that at 12 o'clock (noon) he should begin the bombardment. During the interim…the militia was fast collecting; the town in utmost confusion; the inhabitants removing the sick, the women, children and furniture," Crocker wrote. "About the time

It was James Madison, the country's fourth president, who outlined a list of grievances against the British as the reasons for America's declaration of war in 1812. *Courtesy of the White House Historical Association.*

set the cannonading began, and continued with very little intermission till night. This morning, at sunrise, she sailed westward. Fortunately no lives were lost and no person hurt."

Crocker went on to write that his home had been hit the hardest. "The damage done to houses, outbuildings and salt-works has been considerable... The greatest sufferer was myself, having eight thirty-two pound shot through my house, some through my outbuildings, and many through my saltworks. The greatest part of the furniture in the house was destroyed," he wrote.

## BLACKMAIL OR BOMBS

The captain of the *Nimrod* seemed to take special umbrage at the citizens of Falmouth, one of the few groups to challenge the British control of the coast. But all of Cape Cod was exposed to attacks by the fleet of British warships. The British navy was able to blockade most of the ports along Cape Cod, and any vessel that dared to run supplies or trade goods through the blockade risked being seized and its crew taken prisoner. British sailors raided Cape Cod harbors, seizing or scorching ships at will. Often landing parties ravaged the countryside, stealing crops and livestock and burning down buildings, homes, salt works and businesses. The local militias were all that stood between the British forces and havoc.

British fleet commanders often demanded payment from the various Cape Cod towns in exchange for holding off on an attack. In one case, Admiral Lord Howe sailed the HMS *Newcastle* to Orleans and proclaimed that if the town did not pay $1,000, he would destroy the local salt works. Other Cape towns, including Eastham and Brewster, paid substantial sums to the British to save their salt works. Salt making at the time was an important Cape Cod industry due to the close connection of salt with fishing. Cape Cod was the saltshaker of America. It was the major export and moneymaker of Cape Cod.

Unlike the other Cape towns, the town of Orleans refused the British demand for payment, and the HMS *Newcastle* attacked, but the huge ship was too large and heavy to navigate Orleans' coastal shoals and marshes and was not able to get within firing range of the town. Its cannonballs fell far short of the town and did little if any damage. The local Orleans militia gathered and managed to fight off an attempted British landing and invasion. Several British sailors were killed, the British forces retreated and the town and the precious salt works were saved.

## The Saltshaker of America

During the American Revolution, British blockades of American ports made salt difficult to come by. Salt was an essential product for humans and livestock as a preservative. To make up for this loss, salt works were established all over Cape Cod. The sea provided an endless supply of the mineral, but producing it required vast amounts of seawater to generate even an appreciable amount of salt. It took almost four hundred gallons of seawater and two cords of firewood to produce one bushel of salt. This was hardly cost-effective.

In the beginning, salt was produced by evaporating seawater in huge kettle boilers over a fire. Eventually, large wooden vats were used to contain the seawater, and solar evaporation replaced the wood-burning fires. In order to get enough seawater necessary to produce the salt, windmills were built to pump the salt water to the salt works. Salt was made in a variety of locations along the shores of Buzzards Bay, the first one by Caleb Perry on the southwest side of a large salt pond known as Eel Pond at Monument Beach.

During the British blockade and salt embargo of the War of 1812, it became necessary for Cape Codders to have an independent source. Salt works sprung up in Falmouth and Woods Hole. The sale and exportation of salted codfish was a major industry on Cape Cod, but the salt had to be imported from England and other distant shores until Cape Cod began its own salt production. Although historians most famously hail the British government's tax on tea as one of the causes of the American Revolution, the British also imposed a severe tax on salt. This tax hit the colonists hard.

The Continental Congress became so concerned about the embargo of salt that in 1776, it provided a bonus for each bushel of salt produced. Those engaged in the manufacture of salt were awarded thirty-three cents.

## Return

In June 1814, the *Nimrod* and the *Superb* returned to Buzzards Bay. Wareham was a perfect target for the British warships because it was a center of shipbuilding and iron. It was known that Wareham was involved with privateering during the war. It was also rumored that Wareham was hiding a fleet of Falmouth-based ships. Sighting the warships off the coast of Mattapoisett, Ebenezer Bourne set out to warn the inhabitants of Wareham with his cries of, "The British are coming! The British are coming!"

And they did. The HMS *Nimrod* sailed with six barges carrying two hundred troops and landed at Long Wharf, where the Narrows Bridge is located today. The *Nimrod* and other British warships had been busy wreaking havoc along the New England coast. According to the *Compilation of Reports on Committee of Foreign Relations, United States Senate, 1789–1901*:

> *In January 1814 the British brig* Nimrod *anchored off the wharf in Barnstable demanded the field pieces and other property there and threatened in case of refusal to fire upon the town. In March Falmouth was bombarded. June 11 barges from two British ships of war entered Scituate Harbor burned several vessels and carried off others. On the 17th of the same month a British ship of war two brigs and several small craft came to anchor near Scituate Harbor and on the 9th of July a contribution of provisions demanded of Scituate by the British ship* Nymph *was resisted by the militia. In June again barges from the enemy's ships appeared at the entrance of Cohasset Harbor and burned a coasting sloop. There being a large amount of shipping at the wharves the militia were called out…*

## THE HEART OF THE PATRIOT

In an article published in the September 6, 1834 issue of the Dedham, Massachusetts newspaper, the *Norfolk Advertiser*, an unnamed author recounted the Wareham attack twenty years later.

> *Among the events of the last war, the attack on Wareham is one which ought not to be forgotten. Time does its work in obliterating a recollection of that period when all was dark and dreary; when despondency alone seemed to be triumphant, and business, commerce and manufactures, were engulfed in one common ruin. The heart of the patriot was chilled by the disasters which came o'er our land and the hopes of the brave frozen by the supineness of our rulers. Now, that war, famine or a pestilence have long since left our borders and given way to the hum of industry and enterprise, it is well to look back upon those scenes which moved the heart of the patriot, and made sad the hopes of the strong*

*"An Old Song of Courage"*
*Then, warriors on shore, be brave,*
*Your wives and homes defend;*
*Those precious boons be true to save,*
*And hearts and sinews bend.*
*Oh, think upon your fathers' fame,*
*For glory marked the way;*
*And this foe aimed the blow,*
*But victory crowned the day.*
*Then emulate the deeds of yore,*
*Let victory crown the day.*
*—from an old song of the period*

# Chapter 2

# NIMROD: THE SCOURGE OF BUZZARDS BAY

*Like Nimrod, a mighty hunter before the Lord.*
*—Genesis 10:11*

Laid down at the Ipswich shipyard in Suffolk, England, in November 1811 by its builder, Jazeb Baily, and completed and launched on May 25, 1812, *Nimrod* was a cruiser-class sloop (differing from vessels of the same design known as Cherokee-class sloops), meaning that it carried sixteen guns on its single deck, all of them carronades (Cherokee-class ships carried ten guns), and was also armed with two six-pounder chaser cannon mounted on the bow, allowing the ship to fire at targets directly ahead. This gave the ship the ability to deliver 262 pounds of solid shot in one broadside—not inconsiderable given that each carronade was hurling a projectile weighing thirty-two pounds (though sixty-eight-pounder carronades were not uncommon on larger ships).

## BUILDING A PREDATOR

*Nimrod* was a typical example of the remarkable blend of simplicity and functionality of design represented in the cruiser-class sloops. It was one hundred feet in length with a keel that ran almost the entire length of its straight-swept hull at seventy-seven feet. The deck was thirty feet, seven inches wide, giving ample room for the operation of the guns, and though small in comparison to merchant vessels of similar design, the ship's hold was twelve feet, ten inches deep with the capacity to transport up to 384 tons of men, powder, ammunition and any other supplies it might need to carry out its mission. Even when encumbered with such weight, it remained astonishingly nimble in the water, drawing only six feet at the bow and eleven feet aft.

Given the amount of firepower mounted on the ship's deck, it could operate extremely close to shore, being very well suited to slipping through the oftentimes narrow and treacherous New England waterways with ease and acting as a sort of floating battery. While larger ships might only be able to come within a quarter mile or more of the shore in many places, *Nimrod* could oftentimes measure that distance in scant yards, greatly enhancing its ability to effectively bombard the shore with deadly and telling accuracy,

as it would soon demonstrate in coming ship-to-ship and ship-to-shore engagements in the waters off Cape Cod.

## BLOCKADE DUTY

After its initial sea trials, the fitting out was finished at the Sheerness Dockyard in North Kent on November 12, 1812. Purposely built for patrolling harbors and ship-to-shore engagements, the *Nimrod* only spent ten more days in England mustering its crew under the command of Nathaniel Mitchell before sailing into the Atlantic to its duty station off the East Coast of the United States. There it was to join the more than forty other frigates, brigs, sloops and ships of the line, essentially cutting New England off from the rest of the world, along with the particularly effective blockading of Massachusetts Bay and Cape Cod. Boston had ceased to exist as a useful port, and though, as will always occur, some ships managed to slip through the British blockade, Boston was cut off so as to render the city tactically subdued, and it was considered so for the majority of the war.

## BRITISH SHIPS IN AMERICAN WATERS

The design of the *Nimrod* was a direct continuation of a naval arms race between the British and French that had been going on since the seventeenth century. While the ebb and flow of the types of vessels and how and where they were employed is beyond the scope of this work, in general terms, the most common ships in use during the blockade of the U.S. coast and the attack on Wareham, in addition to frigates, brigs and sloops, were British "ships of the line" (so named for the naval tactic of lining up ships to deliver as large a broadside at the enemy line as possible). These were divided into several classes based on their sail configuration and number of guns.

The HMS *Nimrod* was a remarkably well-designed ship that was both nimble and carried considerable firepower. It was one of the most often built types of British warship. *Courtesy of Falmouth Historical Society.*

The largest were generally the first-rate ships of the line. These massive vessels had three or more gun decks holding more than one hundred cannon and crews in excess of 800 men. These were generally the types of ships used in blockades (several first-rate ships had blockaded Boston before the Revolution) and large combat actions. Second-rate ships of the line had two to three gun decks on which were arranged between ninety and ninety-eight guns with crews of about 750 men. Cannon could be added to change the class between first and second rate, but gun decks were often kept to two and the number of guns lower to make the ships cheaper and easier to build as well as maintain. Third-rate ships most often had two gun decks (and sometimes one) with anywhere from sixty-four to eighty guns and a crew of 200 to 300 men. As these ships went down in class and size, they were necessarily faster, cheaper to build and more economical for coastal operations, as they could operate closer to land-based targets and take advantage of the myriad natural harbors and hiding places along the New England coast.

## Bristling with Guns

Supporting the larger ships of the line were smaller sloops and brigs, which served as launches and cargo carriers and performed reconnaissance. HMS *Nimrod* was known as a brig-sloop, a compact vessel that had two masts, as opposed to the three masts of a frigate, and was square-rigged (brig-sloops were rigged like larger vessels but had fewer sails). These were extremely popular vessels during the late eighteenth and early nineteenth centuries, as they were cheaper to build, had

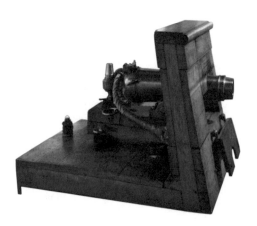

smaller crews and weaponry that required less training and, though they didn't have the cruising endurance or crew and cargo capacity of larger frigates and ships of the line, could still carry considerable firepower.

The carronade sacrificed range and accuracy but allowed for serious close-range hitting power with a smaller crew. It was the "blunderbuss of the sea." *Courtesy of Rama, from the display at Toulon Naval Museum.*

Further, they had a shallow draft (between six and eleven feet), making them ideal for coastal raids. Then, as now, with economics playing a large part in warfare, a great deal of these ships were built by the British, numbering about 110 examples in all, making them one of the most built type of British warship. They were also the most heavily armed, given their size-to-gun ratio.

# THE CARRONADE

Brass carronades (nicknamed "smashers" and named after the Carron Company of Falkirk Scotland, which manufactured them), being compact and yet capable of serious close-range firepower, began to become increasingly popular on British sloops of war, having been observed to have great success in the hands of American mariners both during the Revolution and on various sloops and ships of the line during the Napoleonic Wars. (Ironically, however, due to particular manufacturing requirements for carronades, they were unavailable to the French at that time and would not appear on Gallic ships for several years.) They were considered a cheaper alternative to augment a ship's firepower rather than a main weapon and were seen by the admiralty as such. Further, before this time, carronades were frequently not even counted in the tally of a larger ship's guns (they weren't identified as "guns" as their bore and use placed them somewhere between a mortar and a cannon), so a vessel listed as thirty guns could in actuality have a much greater number, unless the carronades formed the majority or all of a ship's armament, as was the case on smaller or unrated ships.

This type of gun was well suited to both privateer duties and self-defense of commercial shipping of the period, mainly due to its greater ease of handling, abbreviated amount of training for new crews and, perhaps most desirably, the fact that it could be manned by a much smaller gun crew than either a rifle, larger cast-iron cannon or one of the more advanced ship-to-ship weapons available, the Congreve rocket. Carronades were primarily used to destroy an enemy ships rigging but were equally adept at killing large numbers of the crew with a single blast. They fired either large, heavy shot (usually between thirty-two and sixty-eight pounds), bar or chain shot and, frequently, grape shot, essentially turning them into giant shotguns. In one instance, there was a story of a British ship raking a French vessel during the battle of Trafalgar with an entire keg of five hundred musket balls.

The popular conception of naval gunfights of the eighteenth and nineteenth centuries was that ships began to hurl lead and shot at one another on sight as they closed over great distances, masts flying apart, decks raked with splinters and the dead until the terrible moment when they met and battle was truly well joined with pistol and sword in a brutal fight to the finish. While that makes for a great tale, by and large, that's just what they were: tales. While ships of the line might have fought at greater distances, owing to their more accurate cannon and better-trained crews, most privateer engagements and even military actions between enemy sloops took place at much closer distances, oftentimes within one hundred yards, with gun crews holding off firing until they had a much more reasonable—if not guaranteed—chance at hitting their targets. Given that the guns had rudimentary sights, if any at all, hitting the target entailed a good amount of guesswork. In fact, many engagements were decided by one volley. Maritime history has several examples in which opposing ships held their fire until close enough that a single volley from one vessel was enough to convince another that further action would not be advantageous, if it had not already suffered serious, even mortal damage in the first discharge. And while ships' crews did board other vessels and fight hand to hand, it was by far the exception rather than the rule. Eventually, however, the increased quality of rifled cannon would see the range of engagements enlarged by placing heavier emphasis on accurate long-range fire and carronades would gradually disappear from the decks of warships, having been completely replaced by around the 1850s.

## SEA SHANTIES

Sea shanties were popular onboard songs for British and American seamen. Since everything onboard ship was done by the crews, which were the only source of power for rigging sails, rowing and other functional enterprises, the singing of sea shanties actually served a useful purpose. The rhythm of the song synchronized the labor of the crew members as they went about their arduous duties. Shanties also had a communal purpose. The singing helped alleviate the boredom and diminished the load of hard work.

Most shanties are "call and response" songs, with one voice, that of the shantyman, singing the verse while the other sailors sing the responses. A simple example includes the following from the shanty "Boney."

*Shantyman singing: Boney was a warrior,*
*Sailors responding: Way, hey, ya!*
*Shantyman singing: A warrior and a terrier,*
*Sailors responding: Jean-François!*

The shantyman was a sailor who led the others in singing. He was usually self-appointed. A sailor would not generally sign on as a shantyman but took on the role in addition to his other work on board. Sailors believed to be good shantymen were valuable and respected. It was a good professional skill to have, along with strong arms and back.

Historically, shanties were usually not sung ashore, although today they are part of the popular music culture. One of the most popular British shanties was "What Shall We Do with the Drunken Sailor?"

*What will we do with a drunken sailor?*
*What will we do with a drunken sailor?*
*What will we do with a drunken sailor?*
*Early in the morning!*
*Way hay and up she rises,*
*Way hay and up she rises,*
*Way hay and up she rises,*
*Early in the morning!*
*Put him in a long boat till he's sober,*
*Put him in a long boat till he's sober,*
*Put him in a long boat till he's sober,*
*Early in the morning!*

## Leading the Mission

*Nimrod* came under the command of Sir Alexander Inglis Cochrane, commander in chief of the North American Station. Alexander, whose father was the eighth Earl of Dundonald, was the youngest of six sons, and being quite unlikely to ever inherit the peerage, he pursued a military career. While his eldest brother inherited his father's title, the remaining brothers were quite familiar with fighting in the Americas. His elder brother Charles (who had been married to a daughter of Major John Pitcairn, killed at the Battle of Bunker Hill) was killed in the siege of Yorktown during

The Battle of Waterloo in June 1815, perhaps one of the most famous battles in history, was the final undoing of Napoleon. Though an enormous battlefield with almost 200,000 combatants on both sides, it was nonetheless representative of the size of many battles fought during the Napoleonic Wars and illustrative of just how draining it was on the resources of the countries of Europe. *Courtesy of Library of Congress.*

the American Revolution. Two other brothers held important positions in the army and navy, and though quite active, they were not known as being completely honorable. In fact, the Earl of St. Vincent was known to have said of the family: "The Cochranes are not to be trusted out of sight. They are all mad, romantic, money-getting and not truth-telling—and there is not a single exception in any part of the family."

Assigned to the Buzzard's Bay area with orders to pay particular attention to Onset Bay and the Wareham River, both believed to be major harboring points for privateers attacking British shipping, the *Nimrod* joined the seventy-four-gun third-rate frigate *Superb* under the command of Captain Charles Paget, chief officer of the squadron stationed off the coast of New London, Connecticut, tasked with keeping the lower Cape under tight control. Though only thirty-six years old at the time, Paget had considerable experience of the sea, having served in the Royal Navy since he was twelve. Like Cochrane, he was also a younger son in a high-ranking family (his elder brother was first marquis of Anglesey, who lost a leg fighting at the Battle of

Waterloo) and demonstrated early on a keen ability to size up opponents and react decisively in battle.

Paget earned command of his first vessel, HMS *Martin*, by the age of nineteen and won several decisive victories over French and Spanish vessels in the Bay of Biscay and in the Mediterranean, taking a number of prizes, ranging from military vessels to treasure galleons, and rising steadily through the ranks. And while he was known for his considerable martial abilities, he was also noted to be a consummate professional in his treatment of captured enemy crews. He never conducted himself in a cruel or barbarous fashion (many officers of the time did not measure up to such distinction) and was in fact quite chivalrous, frequently going out of his way to ensure that every reasonable effort would be made to preserve life and prevent its unnecessary loss.

## Guarding a World Empire

Paget could not, however, claim that he was against the practice of the impressment of American sailors, both because he, like many British officers and members of the upper class, felt that despite the loss of the colonies in the Revolution, Americans were destined to fail in governing themselves and were still essentially British subjects that could be brought back into the fold. Secondly, being a naval officer, he was keenly aware of the drainage of manpower in the navy due not only to commitments abroad but also to attrition suffered in the fighting with France, and replacements had to come from somewhere.

Despite the fact that the British had such a reputation for well-trained fighting men and had quite literally the most powerful navy in the world, it was the very position of that nation that was problematic when it came to guarding and maintaining a worldwide empire. Indeed, one of the more simplified reasons America entered into the war (beyond legal or moral notions of commercial rights and sovereignty) was that the British were not just stopping American commerce and stealing its goods and ships but stealing its crews as well.

If one has ever seen a traditional sailing vessel in action, even a small, single-masted sailboat, it's very clear that it takes a great deal of labor, both skilled and unskilled, to operate the ship effectively. And naturally, the larger a ship, the more men it took to crew properly. Most seagoing ships required dozens of different specialties in addition to basic labor to remain at sea, maintain the

*Above*: Impressment refers to the act of taking men into a navy by force and with or without notice. It was used by the Royal Navy in wartime as a way of supplying crews for warships. *Courtesy Library of Congress.*

*Left*: Charles Paget (1778–1839) was the son of an earl and had a distinguished naval career, eventually becoming a rear admiral and commander in chief on the coast of Ireland. He was also a member of Parliament, though he did not make any significant contributions there. He died of yellow fever at sea while traveling to Jamaica. *Courtesy Edward Clarence Paget (1913). Memoir of the Hon'ble Sir Charles Paget, G.C.H., 1778–1839.*

vessel and deal with emergencies. In order to become a competent seaman, one had to sail for a good deal of time in order to understand the workings of the ship. One cannot become a competent blacksmith, carpenter, sail maker or any other occupation, for that matter, overnight. It's a simple fact that it takes time to learn new skills, and a great number of these skills were needed on sailing vessels. In a time when the occupation of a father was a strong predictor of his children's path in life, a large enough pool of the skilled laborers needed to operate the navy simply didn't exist, even in a nation with a strong maritime tradition. Further, serving king and country was not a particularly attractive option in the nineteenth century.

Conditions onboard Royal Navy ships, for the ordinary seaman, were unpleasant at best and not infrequently intolerable the majority of the time. Ships were crowded, disease was rampant, food was barely worthy of being called such and death was a constant companion, never far off and from a great variety of sources. Coupled with relentlessly tedious and repetitive duty for extremely poor pay, it's no wonder that the navy did not attract the best and brightest. In fact, it was more often seen as an extension of the penal system, with the majority of ships being crewed with debtors, thieves and murderers avoiding prison in many cases. This is, by and large, why smaller ships whose crews could be interchanged or replaced easily were attractive to the admiralty. Taking the carronade discussed earlier is a good example of why a weapon that required a smaller crew and less training to operate was attractive.

The British navy was well known and even feared for its reliance on tough, repetitive drill given under the eye of demanding taskmasters who expected sailors to learn quickly. Mistakes could bring not only severe punishment but, in action, could spell disaster for a gun crew that did not follow the precise steps necessary for the operation of the piece. An accident when handling large charges of gunpowder could instantly endanger an entire ship, and so the necessity of a gun crew to be able to operate its weapon, especially under the duress of combat, was essential. When a crew was well trained in the loading and firing of their gun, they simply had little time to contemplate their possibly imminent death or the hellish environment of a gun deck.

Shouting men, choking smoke, screaming wounded, terrible heat and numerous mishaps where the recoil of a gun would cause it to roll over and horridly mangle the feet of men who frequently took off their shoes in the oppressive atmosphere were all par for the course in heavy action. Further, the firing of cannon is not a simple endeavor in which powder and shot are stuffed in a tube and fired. If any type of heavy weapon is not used by a crew trained in its proper use, beyond the most basic mishaps that could occur, such as missing the target or failure of the piece to discharge, an improperly loaded weapon could explode or recoil in such an erratic fashion as to prove more dangerous to the ship and gunners than their targets.

## FATE OF THE IMPRESSED

It is, therefore, not difficult to see why the navy had to rely on the use of press gangs to keep up their quotas. A global force of thousands of ships required tens of thousands of sailors and other specialized workers to keep things running efficiently. It was a benefit, however, that most ships serving in the Americas did not have impressed crews, who would have simply jumped ship and gone home. Rather, most Americans who were taken off their vessels to serve in the Royal Navy were sent to far-off places such as India or the

The impressment of seamen from American ships caused serious tensions between Britain and the United States in the years leading up to the War of 1812. *Courtesy of Vaisseau de Ligne, Time Life, 1979.*

Orient (which is the origin of the term "shanghaied"). This served as a form of insurance against desertion, as even if the sailors were able to escape from the British ships, they would find themselves in a far off land where they did not speak the language, didn't have any money and hence had no mobility— not that they would have much chance in any case, as it was a common practice to lock those not on duty below decks where they could be more closely guarded by the marines. Secondly, even if they were able to make good their escape, in all actuality, any ship on which they could arrange for passage had a high probability that it would be stopped approaching the American coast by a man-of-war, and woe to the sailor who was found out to have deserted. In general, sloops of war did not receive impressed crews unless they were sent to some far-flung station, mainly because of their smaller size and the fact that they did not carry troops who could be spared to guard against desertion. Given these factors, impressment was a frightening prospect because once a man was in British possession, he likely would not leave it again.

*Chapter 3*

# THE SETTLEMENT
# OF WAREHAM

*That house which, loath a rule to break,*
*Served Heaven but one day in the week;*
*Open the rest for all supplies*
*Of news and politics and lies.*
—McFingal: A Modern Epic Poem. Or, The Town Meeting,
*by John Trumbull*

*N*epinnaeKekit, or "Summer Home," is the Wampanoag Indian phrase that appears on the Wareham, Massachusetts town seal. The Wampanoags came to Wareham every summer to take advantage of the plentiful shellfishing and the wild cranberries. The town was officially incorporated on July 10, 1739, by legislative act and included South Wareham, Wareham Center, the Narrows and a portion of Rochester, which is now West Wareham. On August 6 of that year, the first Wareham town meeting was called. Wareham and Onset Village are a tourist attraction and a "summer home" to people all over the country and around the world.

## SETTLEMENT

The town was first settled in 1678 and incorporated as a town in 1739. It combined a portion of Rochester and the western part of Plymouth, known as "the Agawam Plantation," which is currently East Wareham. At the time of the incorporation of Wareham in July 1739, its population is not known. Every town containing forty qualified voters was entitled to a representative in the General Court, but for forty years after incorporation, the town stated that it was not qualified to send a representative, and when it wished to be heard at General Court, it sent an agent instead.

In 1838, Attorney Silvanus Bourne wrote several articles about the town, published by Stillman B. Pratt & Co., in Middleboro, Massachusetts, in 1867. According to Bourne, "The east part of the town, known as the 'Agawam purchase,' lay in the township of Plymouth, and the west part belonged to Rochester, until in 1739, these two tracts were incorporated as the Town of Wareham, the name being borrowed from an old English town, once of some note."

Wareham was enlarged in 1827 to include a portion of the town of Carver known as Tihonet. "From 1739, until 1824, the people of the West end, and the inhabitants of Agawam, were mutually jealous of each other's' rights, so much so that two constables, and two collectors, were always appointed, and even two sets of tax bills were always made," Bourne wrote. The tract of land was originally leased in 1678 for a seven-year period, and in 1682, it was sold by the Town of Plymouth to ten Wareham purchasers, including John Chubbuck, Samuel Bates and John Fearing.

Wareham's modern-day boundaries include the towns of Carver and Plymouth to the north, Bourne to the east, Marion and Rochester to the west, Middleborough along the northern corner and Buzzard's Bay to the south.

## THE ACT OF INCORPORATION

According to the *History of Plymouth County, Massachusetts: With Biographical Sketches of Many of Its Pioneers and Prominent Men* by D. Hamilton Hurd, published in 1884, Wareham's incorporation was signed by J. Quincy, Speaker of the Massacusetts House of Representatives, on July 6, 1739: "In 1739, July 6. This Bill having been read three times in the House of

Representatives, passed to be Enacted." Incorporation documents were signed by the governor on July 10, 1739: "1739, July 10. By His Excellency the Governor I Consent to the Enacting this Bill. J. Belcher."

The incorporation called for the dividing of the towns of Rochester and Plymouth and "erecting a new Town there by the name of Wareham."

According to the incorporation documents: "Whereas the Inhabitants of the East End of the Town of Rochester, and the Inhabitants of a Plantation called Agawam in the Town of Plymouth by Reason of great Difficulties they labor under have addressed this Court, that they may be set off a distinct and separate Township, and vested with all Powers and Privileges that other Towns in this Province are vested with. For which they have obtained the Consent of the said Towns of Rochester and Plymouth."

At the time the incorporation was passed, the Massachusetts General Court ordered Edward Bumpus to call the first town meeting, which was held on August 6, 1739. At the meeting, Bumpus was chosen moderator, Jonathan Hunter was chosen town clerk and Jireh Swift, Jeremiah Bumpus and Jonathan Hunter were chosen as selectmen and assessors.

According to the third Congregational church minister, Reverend Noble Warren Everett, who provided a history of Wareham in Hurd's *History of Plymouth County*, "The size form and architecture of the first meeting house erected in Wareham to the incorporation of the town cannot be ascertained

According to Everett, in 1742 the town voted to buy land from Isaac Bump to build a new meetinghouse:

*This vote indicates that many went to meeting who had no seats and accommodated themselves in the public and by-places with chairs, stools, blocks, etc., and when the town voted to clear them no doubt they made provision for the poor and let the penurious provide for themselves.*

*In 1770, the town voted to give certain subscribers the old meeting house build a new one with and voted to receive the new one on condition that the town keep it in repair and use it for a town house.*

# Buzzards Bay

The Atlantic Ocean's Buzzards Bay is about twenty-eight miles long and eight miles wide. During the early colonial period, the bay was not connected to the Cape Cod Bay that lies to the northeast. It was not until 1914 that the two bays were connected by the Cape Cod Canal. It was named Buzzards Bay by the early colonists, who witnessed a large bird swooping over the shoreline and mistakenly thought it was a buzzard. It turned out to be an osprey. The osprey population along Buzzards Bay and in Wareham has significantly grown thanks to the many efforts of environmentalists concerned with preserving the bird. It is one of North America's largest birds of prey. A fish-eating hawk, the osprey has a white-crested head. It weighs approximately three to four pounds and has a wingspan of up to six feet. There has been a "tremendous resurgence and occurs virtually worldwide, near coastlines, lakes, and rivers, where the birds hunt for their food," according to the National Audubon Society.

# Topography

Wareham, known as the "Gateway to Cape Cod," is the innermost town on the north shore of Buzzards Bay. The town is west of Cape Cod; eighteen miles east of New Bedford; approximately forty-five miles east of Providence, Rhode Island; and fifty-five miles southeast of Boston.

There are several harbors and coves that jut up into the town, creating several peninsulas and providing a winding shoreline. There is approximately 18,550 acres with more than 4,000 acres of dedicated forests. Most of the land is sandy and level, with a few low hills. The highest elevations of the town include Bourne's Hill and Tempest Knob. Bourne's Neck is located at the farthest southeast part of the town. On the east side is Cohasset Narrows, and to the west, near the center of the town, is Wareham Narrows. The southern boundary of Myles Standish State Forest is concurrent with the town line between Wareham and Plymouth. There are fifty-seven miles of coastline along Buzzards Bay and the numerous rivers, lakes and ponds adjacent to the town.

The Wankinco River flows north into Wareham Village, where it turns into the Wareham River, creating the town's main harbor. Easterly is the Agawam River, with its source located in the town of Plymouth.

Wareham's early business and industry included shipbuilding, salt production, iron ore manufacturing, nail production and cranberry farming. It is home of the Tremont Nail Factory, the oldest nail manufacturer in the country. The factory was established in 1819. The first cotton factory in Wareham was built in 1812.

Also because of its beaches and other amenities, it has been a resort town, with many smaller resort areas dispersed through the town, especially in Onset. Historically, its waterways, especially Buttermilk Bay, were once considered as possible routes for the Cape Cod Canal. The canal, which opened on a limited basis in July 1914, was completed in 1916. It goes through Bourne and Sandwich, passing through from Cape Cod Bay to Buzzards Bay just south of the town.

# A BRIEF HISTORICAL PERSPECTIVE

Wareham Historical Commission members Malcolm Phinney and Barbara Bailey gave presentations on Wareham's history to several sets of high school students, with Phinney explaining that glacial washout deposits left behind what is known as the "Wareham pitted plain," which consists of sand and gravel with depressions left by slow-melting chunks of ice as glaciers receded. According to Phinney, the depressions are known as "kettle holes" that were filled with organic matter that led to the formation of bogs.

"Within these bogs, through deposition and an oxidation process, a type of iron ore called bog iron was formed. Early colonists discovered this bog iron, dug it out of the bogs and smelted it into iron, leading to the iron industry in Wareham," Phinney reported.

Although Wareham had a long and successful iron history, when the iron industry died out, many Wareham farmers discovered they could grow cranberries in the bogs.

According to Phinney, waterways, rivers and streams were important to the growth and industry of the town because they could be dammed up and used as a source of power. The two historians said that there had once been an "impressive whaling and shipbuilding industry in Wareham," along with the production of iron.

The Wampanoag Indians were among the first settlers of the area, and they reportedly gave names to some of the town's rivers, many of which are still used today. The Wampanoag name *Weweantic*, given to the Wareham River, means "crooked river," while the name *Agawam* meant a location abundant with fish. *Tihonet*, another Wampanoag name, means "the place of the crane."

"They used to come here for summer," Phinney said of the Wampanoags. "They went inland for the winter months, just like the tourists do."

According to Phinney and Bailey, the Indians would travel from Rhode Island to Plymouth, traveling through Wareham on the way to their destination: "They

The Fearing Tavern, which is maintained as a museum, dates back to the late 1600s. Additions were made in 1765 and 1820. *Courtesy of Michael Vieira.*

would come from Mary's Pond Road in Rochester down what is now Fearing Hill Road to Main Street and then they would connect to [what is now] Route 28 by Elm Street. Somewhere in the vicinity of Red Brook Road, they would split off to the north to Plymouth or continue east to Sandwich." This was an "approximate route," since "back then, it was just a path through the forest."

Historical residences in the town included the Elbridge Fearing House, located just east of the intersection of Blackmore Pond and Fearing Hill Roads.

"The Fearings were an important family in town," Bailey said, adding that members of the Fearing family married into other influential town families.

The Fearing Tavern in Wareham dates back to 1690, Phinney reported.

"This became a very important stagecoach stop. It was a place where the important people in town met and made decisions about the town," he said. The Fearing Tavern also served as a courthouse back in the early years of Wareham. Someone found guilty of such "crimes" as spitting or swearing in public, missing church or being a drunkard might find himself locked in the stocks. Phinney said, "It was public humiliation."

For a guilty verdict for something a bit more serious, such as stealing or getting into a fight, there was the whipping post. Anyone deemed guilty of murder was taken to Plymouth to be hanged.

The current Decas School in Wareham is built on what was once a "muster field," the place where soldiers went to train and prepare for war. As Phinney explained, "Wareham had a group of Minutemen who served in the Revolutionary War."

Phinney reported, "Onset did not contribute to Wareham in the early years. It was not good for agriculture, and the harbor wasn't deep enough for the big boats." But according to Phinney, Onset became a boon for tourists. One of the most popular draws, besides the beach, was the Colonial Casino, where the big bands played and vaudeville was performed.

"Onset then became very important to Wareham," Phinney said.

# ONSET VILLAGE

The picturesque village of Onset is often referred to as "Onset the Beautiful." Its streets are lined with cottages that overlook a sandy white beach adjacent to a tranquil bay. The Indian name *Onset* means the "Sandy Landing Place." It was originally known as Pine Point and became known as Onset after the Onset Bay Grove Association purchased it in 1877. The association was a group of businessmen who were looking for a location to build a spiritual summer camp, but Onset was a hard place to get to because of its thickly forested land and narrow dirt roads. In 1884, a road was built into Onset, and the completion of it led to the small village's growth in tourism. It became an ideal and well-known vacation spot for families. Hotels and rooming houses were built, and new businesses and eateries lined the main thoroughfare.

Although spiritualism and Onset were intertwined, its image was smeared by *The Vampires of Onset*, published by the New England News Co. of Boston. The book was composed of a series of articles by several newspaper reporters exposing fakery in the spiritualist world. Ironically, not a single incident in the book took place in Onset. After the book was published, the Onset Bay Grove Camp Meeting Co., made up of spiritualists who wanted to retain the Indian heritage of spirit guides, was established. A decision was made to worship the Indian native spiritual guides. The group believed this would dispel the negative image *The Vampires of Onset* had given the village. The wigwam was dedicated to the Wampanoag Indians. The Onset Bay Grove Camp Meeting Co. believed that it gave an image of natural, holistic spirituality and would help revitalize Onset's image of spirituality, which it did.

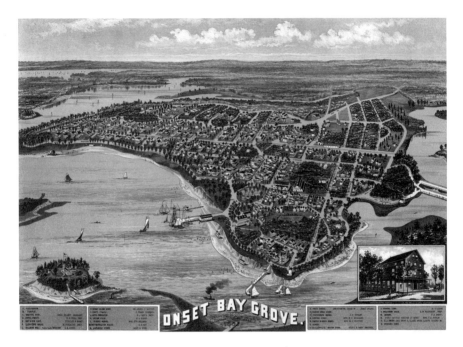

The picturesque village of Onset is often referred to as "Onset the Beautiful." The Indian name *Onset* means "Sandy Landing Place." *Courtesy of Library of Congress.*

The Oniset wigwam still stands today. Above its front door is a plaque that reads, "Erected to the Memory of the Redman—1894—Liberty Throughout the World and Freedom to All Races." It is listed as one of the town's Historical Society monuments.

According to its website, onisetwigwam.com, "Spiritualism is the Science, Philosophy and Religion of continuous life, based upon the demonstrated fact of communication, by means of medium ship, with those who live in the Spirit World. A Spiritualist is one who believes, as the basis of his or her religion, in the communication between this and the spirit world by means of medium ship, and who endeavors to mold his or her character and conduct in accordance with the highest teachings derived from such communion."

Services there center on the wigwam, an octagonal wooden edifice designed to resemble an Indian teepee, which has been an Onset landmark for more than a century. It is the oldest National Spiritualist Camp in the country to have religious services in this type of building.

The reputation of Onset Village was tainted again in 1946 when a Cambridge woman, Ruth McGurk, was murdered. She was reportedly abducted from one of Onset's dance halls. The village was devastated, and the murder hit its tourism industry hard. No one was ever convicted of the crime, and for a time, people were afraid to go out. This only added to the negative image that Onset was starting to garner.

The perspective of Onset changed over the years, and it became better known for its drinking, gambling and dancing establishments, leaving the once spiritual image behind. Much of Onset's growth had been in eating and drinking establishments. Onset had become a party town full of bars. This negative image would stay for many years. In 1960, when the Interstate 195 highway was built, Wareham, Onset and Buzzards Bay were bypassed. The Route 6 businesses in all three towns felt the loss of business.

Onset did rebound and in 1987, when a group of business professionals purchased the small, town-owned golf course and surrounding property and built a country club and twenty-five condominiums. The Bay Pointe Village and Country Club greatly revitalized the area.

Another contributor to the revitalization of Onset was Len Cubellis. In 1988, he bought and refurbished the Onset Pointe Inn and subsequently purchased and refurbished another twenty-three buildings. He was instrumental in creating the Onset Bay Association, the organization responsible for continuing to promote tourism in the town. All of these various improvements have helped make Onset a thriving summer tourist attraction.

## SOLDIERS AND SAILORS MONUMENT

Before Wareham's Soldiers and Sailors Monument on Town Green was erected, Center Park was a town-owned meadow where anyone could bring their livestock to graze. It wasn't until 1902 that a special committee was formed to work with the veterans in town to build the monument. After the Spanish-American War in the late 1890s, Wareham had the present Soldiers and Sailors Monument erected. In 1904, a vote was passed "to erect a Soldiers and Sailors Monument at Center Park and money be raised by borrowing 5,000 dollars for payment of same." According to the Wareham celebration committee report, "In 1906, a vote was passed to purchase and install a flag staff and flag. Two Civil War cannons, each weighing between seven and eight tons, were placed at the foot of the monument. A pyramid of 35 round cannon balls was placed on the east side in front of the cannons. The monument stands today."

"Later, a meeting house was built on the site, but it's no longer there," Malcolm Phinney said. It was made of granite and dedicated in 1905. Bronze plaques on the monument's base list Wareham citizens who served in America's wars, including the French and Indian War, the American Revolution, the War of 1812 and the Civil War. There are also memorials dedicated to those who lost their lives in World War I and World War II, the Korean War and Vietnam.

# RELIGION

Religion always played an important part in the lives of the early settlers, and Wareham was no different. The Wareham First (Congregational) Church was founded soon after the town was incorporated. For nearly one hundred years, this was the only church in town. The first settled minister was Rowland Thatcher, ordained in 1740. His successors included Josiah Cotton, 1774; Noble Everett, 1784–1820; Daniel Hemmenway, 1821–1828; Samuel Nott, ordained 1829; Homer Barrows; and Reverend T.F. Clary.

The Roman Catholics have been in town since before 1865. A building on High Street was purchased by the Catholics that year. This parish has continued to the present time as St. Patrick's Church.

The Baptists were active from about 1830 to 1865, when their church was sold to the Roman Catholics.

The Methodists have been active since about 1831 and, at times, have had churches in the Wareham Center, East Wareham, Onset and Oak Grove sections of town. In the 1960s, the first three were combined into the Wesley United Methodist Church, located on Main Street in Wareham Center.

The Episcopalians began a ministry in Wareham in 1868 but did not become well established until 1883, when the present church building was purchased and moved to Wareham from West Springfield. This church is located on High Street.

The Advent Christian Church, in the Tihonet section of town, was established in 1887.

# WICKETS ISLAND

Wickets Island is a five-acre landmass in Onset Harbor in Wareham. According to Craig S. Chartier, the director of the Plymouth Archaeological Rediscovery Project, "The island was likely once connected to the mainland by an isthmus of sand on its northeast edge. Over time this isthmus was eroded through, eventually creating the island as it is today. "

People may have gone to the island to plant, fish or collect shellfish, but it is unlikely that anyone lived there for extended periods of time because there doesn't appear to be any source of fresh water available on the island.

Early historical maps indicate that Wickets Island belonged to Jabez Wicket, a Native American living in Wareham. According to Chartier, it appears that the Town of Wareham acknowledged that the natives had a rightful claim to the island.

After the death of Jabez Wicket, the island and all improvements on it are believed to have been granted to Jesse Webquish, another Native American. Both Wicket and Webquish fought in the French and Indian War (1754–1763). In the 1800s, the town fathers decided to allow Wicket's Island to be let out for planting."This indicates that the Native owners of the island had either moved away or died and that the island was uninhabited," Chartier said.

The island was leased to various individuals throughout the nineteenth century, and in the late nineteenth century, it came into the hands of a family who built the large house that stood there until 1947, when it burned.

The Great September Gale of 1815 is recorded in local lore as having a dramatic effect on Wickets Island. This storm, considered one of the worst New England hurricanes—second only to the 1938 storm—struck Long Island and southern New England on September 23, 1815. Storms of this intensity often flood barrier islands, strip sediments from beaches and deposit them in marshes, lakes and lagoons. According to a Dartmouth, Massachusetts newspaper account from the period, "Dwelling houses in almost every town have been more or less injured, many barns and out houses, and some dwelling houses have been unroofed, and some few blown down."

It is believed that the storm caused what amounted to a tidal wave to rush into the harbor, causing large-scale erosion of Wickets Island. This erosion is believed to have caused a number of natives graves' on the island to be washed away. The island has been owned since 2003 by a developer that plans to build a luxury home there. BRT-Wickets LLC, a subsidiary of BRT General Corp., bought the secluded retreat in 2003 for $625,000 when the previous owner sold it in bankruptcy.

# HISTORICAL SITES

According to the Wareham Historical Society, the Fearing Tavern, maintained as a museum, is one of five properties that fall under the protection and care of the Wareham Historical Society. The other sites include the One Room Schoolhouse, Union Chapel, Old Methodist Meetinghouse and Captain John Kendrick Maritime Museum. The Fearings were an important family in Wareham. Captain Israel Fearing Jr., the eldest militia officer in town during the British attack, rallied his forces and intercepted the invading troops. He was the son of General Israel Fearing, a Revolutionary War hero. During an attempted invasion of Wareham by the British during the Revolutionary War, Fearing was able to repel the enemy forces, and the town was saved from attack.

According to the society:

> *The building contains portions built in 1690, 1765 and 1820. Sixteen period rooms contain authentic eighteenth- and nineteenth-century furnishings, toys, tools and many decorative and useful objects. The major portion of the Georgian Colonial house with its white clapboarded façade was built by tavern keeper Benjamin Fearing in 1765.*
>
> *Isaac Bump operated a gristmill and lived here following King Phillip's War. The original 1690 home contained four rooms, and the original proprietors of the Agawam Plantation met here to conduct business and planning, which resulted in the incorporation of the town of Wareham in 1739. In the 1820s, Benjamin's son Benjamin Haskell Fearing added a new kitchen and the bedroom wing to the house.*

The Old Methodist Meeting House was built in 1835 across the green from the First Congregational Church, which, until then, had been the only house of worship in Wareham since 1739. According to the Wareham Historical Society, "The Meetinghouse was used for a variety of purposes throughout its life, including as a bakery and a laundromat. When it was given to the Wareham Historical Society, the façade was restored to its original state. It is used by the Society for their meetings."

The One-Room Schoolhouse, known as Schoolhouse #6, was originally built on Great Neck in 1825. "It served as the school for residents in that portion of Wareham for 100 years," according to the historical society, and it was used by the residents of Great Neck for church services until a chapel was built: "During the latter 1800s, a kitchen was added by the Union Chapel

The plaque commemorates that gallantry of the Revolutionary War hero Israel Fearing. During an attempted invasion of Wareham by the British during the Revolutionary War, Fearing was able to repel the enemy forces. *Courtesy of Schlitzer90 (own work) [CC-BY-SA-3.0 (http://creativecommons.org/licenses/by-sa/3.0)], via Wikimedia Commons.*

Association of Great Neck so that other community events could be more easily held in this building. The Schoolhouse was moved from Great Neck to its present location next to the Old Methodist Meeting House on Main Street by the Wareham Historical Society in the 1970s."

The Union Chapel was built around 1880 as a nondenominational place of worship for the times when the weather made it difficult to travel to Wareham Center. "The Union Chapel Association of Great Neck was formed and the original list of subscribers and the money they each contributed toward the cost is available for viewing in the Chapel," according to the historical society. The Wareham Historical Society moved the chapel to its present location next to the schoolhouse and the Old Methodist Meeting House on Main Street in Wareham.

A mile down Main Street from the meetinghouse, schoolhouse and chapel, and overlooking the Narrows Historic District of Wareham, is the Captain John Kendrick House and Maritime Museum. The home was purchased by Captain Kendrick, along with the wharf across the street, in 1778. It is a gambrel-roofed Cape-style house with a center chimney which was built around 1745. The original paneling and other architectural features remain intact, and the Wareham Historical Society has maintained the early wallpapers and furnishings from the eighteenth and nineteenth centuries. Inside are many items honoring the maritime history of Wareham. According to the historical society, "Following the residency of the Kendricks, the home retained its importance in the town, having the post office within it, as well as being the home of other important Wareham residents, including the famed maritime artist, Charles Sidney Raleigh." The Wareham Historical Society began operating this building as a maritime museum in 1976.

The Captain John Kendrick House and Maritime Museum is a gambrel-roofed Cape-style house with a center chimney that was built around 1745. *Courtesy of Michael Vieira.*

Kendrick became the first American to sail into the closed nation of Japan. Japan had been in self-imposed isolation, shutting out all foreigners for 150 years until Kendrick arrived at Kushimoto on the south coast in May 1791. According to Scott Ridley, author of the much acclaimed book *Morning of Fire: John Kendrick's Daring American Odyssey in the Pacific*:

> *The journey to Japan was just one small part of Kendrick's efforts to establish an American presence in the Pacific. At this point in history the world powers were vying for control of the North Pacific and its trade routes. The Spanish had been granted dominion over the Pacific by Pope Alexander VI in 1493. For more than three hundred years it was known in Europe as the "Spanish Lake," jealously guarded by Spanish warships. Now Russia and Britain were seeking to break Spain's hold. Kendrick sailed into the midst of the fight that was brewing.*
>
> *Leaving Boston with two ships in October 1787 he sailed around the treacherous Cape Horn. His mission was to open a fur trade between the Pacific Northwest Coast and China, discover the Northwest Passage, and establish an American outpost on the Pacific coast of North America. He*

*ended up running a single-ship campaign to hold off both the British and the Spanish. As part of his efforts, Kendrick built alliances with native people in the Hawaiian Islands and on the Pacific Northwest coast and armed them with muskets.*

*In 1792, Kendrick purchased more than one thousand square miles of land on what is now Vancouver Island from his native allies. He forwarded copies of his deeds to then Secretary of State Thomas Jefferson, saying he believed the purchase would prove of great benefit to the young nation. A dozen years later, Lewis and Clark would set off on their landmark journey. When they reached the Pacific, they camped on the banks of the Columbia River, named after Kendrick's command ship.*

According to Ridley, "Kendrick opened a gateway to the Pacific for American ships around Cape Horn. His other actions set the stage for the era to come. Kendrick died at the hands of the British at Honolulu in December 1794. His widow, Huldah Pease Kendrick, went on to live for several years in the house at the Narrows that now serves as a museum. She never knew the full story of what had happened to her husband, or what he had achieved."

# Chapter 4
# WAR ALONG THE COAST

A Nation Unprepared—Muddled Objectives—New England's
Maritime War—The Cork in the Bottle—A Coast under Siege—
*Nimrod* Joins the Fight

*Our ships all in motion once whitened the ocean*
*They sailed and returned with a cargo.*
*Now doomed to decay*
*they have fallen a prey*
*To Jefferson worms and embargo.*
*—1808 Newburyport newspaper*

By the time the War of 1812 began, the United States had only existed as a country for about twenty-nine years, and very unlike the foreign policy of the Republic today, for a good deal of time, we were a fairly xenophobic state. Entanglement in foreign affairs was a sort of rule number one on our political "don't" list for a number of reasons, among them at the time that militarily, we lacked an army or navy of sufficient size, had a significant want of efficient structure for building and equipping such forces and compared to the seemingly ever-warring Europeans, our dearth of practical experience in the planning and execution of efficient prolonged tactical engagements was pronounced, to say the least.

# A NATION UNPREPARED

Our navy was small and—though competently led—mustered only twenty vessels of all types, while the British, of course, had the largest and most powerful standing navy in the world. America—or, more specifically, New England with its strong maritime tradition—on the other hand, frequently relied on privateers to act as a sort of floating militia to supplement the navy in times of need. While certainly a cheaper alternative to maintaining a full-time professional force, it led to all manner of complications, from varied availability of ships to a pronounced inconsistency in support for (and consequently adherence to) orders, as well as a lack of the sense of duty to stay with the fight until it was concluded. In a military establishment, individual officers and enlisted men don't have the liberty to pick and choose which orders are important or should be followed, while privateers feel they had a much freer hand to do so, which, naturally, could seriously affect the intended outcome of an operation. Though this was an infrequent problem, as privateers performed some of the bravest duties of the war, it still existed nonetheless.

The situation in the army, however, was quite different. Often ill supplied, paid irregularly and led by officers frequently appointed for political reasons, the army was plagued by poor leadership and a general lack of efficient organization. It did not help that it was also a small force. Though Congress had authorized the size of the army to stand at about 35,000 men, when the war commenced, it was barely a third of that size with 11,700 of all ranks protecting the American frontier and scattered throughout a series of forts and posts from Maine to the Great Lakes, down the Mississippi River to Spanish Florida. Once again, there was a strong reliance on the states to supply militia to make up for these deficits, and while more than 400,000 would serve in the course of the war, many never saw front-line action. Unlike the regular army, in which a man's personal opinion didn't factor into whether or not orders were followed, militia often reflected strong regional influences.

Though Congress agreed, albeit grudgingly, to commence hostilities (the decision to go to war passed the senate, and the War of 1812 was largely seen as "Madison's war"), the militia's willingness to fight waxed and waned according to whether or not a region liked or disliked Madison. And while, once again, many individual militia companies had proved to be as brave and resilient as any British army unit during the Revolution, there were numerous examples that had earned them nothing but scorn from

*Left*: The Right Honorable Robert Jenkinson, second Earl of Liverpool (1770–1828), prime minister of England (1812–1827). The son of one of the king's closest advisors, he was the real power behind the throne during the War of 1812. Regarded as a hard and uncompromising man, he nonetheless presided over several important events in the history of his country. *Courtesy of Thomas Lawrence.*

*Below*: An American brig-sloop of the same class as *Nimrod*, as it would appear while underway. They were also in common usage in America as trade vessels and were frequently outfitted as privateers. *Courtesy of James Grant,* The Narrative of a Voyage of Discovery, Performed in His Majesty's Vessel the *Lady Nelson*, of 60 Tons Burthen, with Sliding Keels, in the Years 1800, 1801, and 1802, to New South Wales, *published July 1803.*

the English. Many foreign officers didn't even feel threatened by militia, assuming they would either fail to fire a shot or simply run away at the first sign of danger. Indeed, this had been demonstrated more than once in American conflicts with England; rather than stand and fight in the open, American militia frequently ran away, only to turn and fire from covered or otherwise concealed positions.

While it's temptingly easy to dismiss this as cowardice, it must also be remembered that beyond the European concept of how war was fought— out in the open in orderly ranks, a style that Americans did not adopt nor did they have the manpower for—militia commonly fought closely to the area in which they were mustered, and so beyond the obvious dangers to which soldiers are exposed, such as disease, maiming and the general rigors of campaigning, they also had much more to lose personally, with their families and property being right in the vicinity of the fight. In general, service in the army was an unpopular notion in the early 1800s owing in no small part to the poor pay and general inefficiency of the officers. Further, unlike the professional army, with soldiers drawn from far and wide, militia companies were made up of men from the immediate area, usually the same town, who had intimate knowledge of one another, oftentimes being friends and more frequently related by blood and marriage. They simply fought better in their home states and were reluctant to leave simply for some notion of the greater good of the country. It was this bond that would play a crucial role in how the attack on Wareham played out, coupled with the manner in which the British were executing the war.

# MUDDLED OBJECTIVES

The roots of the War of 1812, unlike the causes of some other conflicts in which the country would be involved, were convoluted and murky, a complicated amalgamation of political and regional intrigues and poor timing, tainted by greed and personal ambition. Indeed, when the war ended, not only had none of the original grievances for which we went to war in the first place been resolved, but also none of the political or military aims were gained. President Madison had been continuing the use of economic sanctions begun under President Jefferson to influence British policy. However, prior to the commencement of hostilities, the British had decided to not only relax the blockading of American vessels but also agreed to halt the policy of impressing American sailors. For England, the war with America was a distinctly secondary theater of operations, being that it had much more pressing concerns at hand and had been heavily engaged in continental fighting for ten years prior to America's declaration of war. Fighting had been raging across Europe for years as Napoleon's armies won battle after battle in his efforts to conquer Europe and expand the power of the French empire. Britain and France had been fighting each other on and off for centuries but had been at peace since signing the Treaty of Amiens in 1802.

However, by May 1803, the treaty had fallen apart, and Britain had once again declared war on France. This one year would actually mark the only period of general peace in Europe until Napoleon abdicated in 1815. At this time, France was considered one of the superpowers in Europe, and it took all of England and its allies' resources to engage. Though England had been able to produce foodstuffs and war materials, it was beginning to rely more and more on the availability of American goods to provision its armies. A poor grain harvest in 1812 coupled with the need to provide more materiel for its troops fighting the Battle of the Peninsula in Spain and Portugal forced England's hand, and the government agreed to relax some of the sanctions it had placed on American shipping. Unfortunately, by this time, it was too late. As it could take up to two months for word to cross the Atlantic in the nineteenth century, Congress and the Senate had agreed to declare war on Britain on June 18, 1812.

# NEW ENGLAND'S MARITIME WAR

The war was fought in three distinct theaters; the Great Lakes and Canadian frontier, the southern states and the Atlantic seaboard, with each region perceiving what it wanted out of the war in a different light. For the people in the southern states, it was possession of Spanish Florida. Those who lived in the Ohio Valley had an eye toward uncontested control of the Great Lakes and perhaps even fully pushing the English out of Canada so that the United States would possess all of North America. In New England, which felt the war in the form of crushing economic sanctions, it was the reestablishment of free trade and the ability for residents to pursue a maritime livelihood as they had before the series of political blunders beginning with the Non-Intercourse Act of 1809 under then president Jefferson, which prohibited all trade with England and France.

Though intended to cause harm to the English and French economies, in actuality, almost overnight it was ruinous to commerce on the Cape and islands, which depended not only on trade with England—their largest and most profitable customer—but also on free access to markets around the world. Now, with the onset of the war, commerce was being stifled by the British blockade. In fact, commerce in New England suffered so badly that the value of its exports decreased 95 percent from about $130 million in 1807 to just $7 million by 1814. What did not help matters was that Britain was the United States' largest trading partner, taking in about 50 percent of all exported goods in general and about 80 percent of American cotton production. And British seizure of American merchant vessels, exclusive of those destroyed, led to the loss of over 1,400 ships, most of which were sent to Nova Scotia or the Caribbean as prizes. For the United States, this was a devastating loss to its mercantile fleet, and while a little over 800 British merchant ships were captured by the U.S. Navy during the war, this represented less than 10 percent of the total British vessels, causing little if any disruption to Britain's ability to maintain trade and lines of supply.

For the citizens of Cape Cod and New England, the main concern was the British tactics used to subdue the ability of the states to conduct trade, maintain their food supply (fishing being the major industry in New England at the time) and guarantee the safety of coastal towns. When Alexander Cochrane arrived off the East Coast of the United States, his first priority was to set up a cordon intended to squeeze the country into submission by controlling all waterways from the Mississippi River to the coast of Maine, with particular emphasis on separating New England from the rest of the country. He felt that if he were able to separate the northern population, among whom the war was unpopular to begin with, and crush their commercial interests, they would use their considerable political weight to either demand an end to the war or, more probably, to fracture the United States by inducing New England to secede. In many ways, he was correct, as the British blockade caused more than political pressure over the loss of profits. It also directly affected the ability of its citizens to survive.

An economic fact of the times was that New Englanders relied heavily on the importation of manufactured goods and foodstuffs, the supply of which had, until recently, been paid for with the exportation of textiles, grain and other raw materials. Now, with little or no goods going in and out of port, the people had no income and a dramatic reduction in the amount of daily necessities available, and owing to the high risk of capture, those who did have ships left were reluctant to risk them by venturing out to fish—the lifeblood of both commerce and food production for the people of Cape Cod. In fact, many communities continued to sell grain and other supplies to Canada despite the law technically prohibiting them from doing so. Some ship owners did fit out vessels as privateers in an effort to attack or capture British ships or run through the blockade, but given that New England was effectively bottled up, they contributed little to the war effort.

## The Cork in the Bottle

Due to the commitments on the British military discussed previously, in late 1812, there were only about forty-five ships of the line and frigates as well as an equal number of smaller vessels and sloops of war available to enforce a blockade against the United States that stretched along both the Gulf and Atlantic seaboards. While not a great number of ships, Vice Admiral Cochrane, who was in command of the North American Station, was well experienced in naval blockade, and he made good use of what was available to him. Arrayed from Maine to the seas off Connecticut and New York, he deployed a force of forty-four ships that until 1814 would turn the northeastern United States into a war zone for any ship brave—or foolhardy—enough to challenge him. Though the makeup and number would change at various points of the war, the force that served as the cork in this bottle was made up of the following vessels:

Ships of the line:
1. HMS *Ramillies* (seventy-four guns), Captain Thomas Masterman Hardy
2. HMS *Albion* (seventy-four guns), Captain Charles Bayne Hodgson Ross, flagship of Admiral Sir George Cockburn
3. HMS *Valiant* (seventy-four guns), Captain Robert Dudley Oliver
4. HMS *Sceptre* (seventy-four guns), Captain Charles B.H. Ross, flagship of Admiral Sir George Cockburn, early 1814
5. HMS *Victorious* (seventy-four guns), Captain John Talbot
6. HMS *La Hogue* (seventy-four guns), Captain Thomas Blayden Capel
7. HMS *Bulwark* (seventy-four guns), Captain David Milne
8. HMS *Superb* (seventy-four guns), Captain Charles Paget, flagship of Admiral Henry Hotham, 1814–15
9. HMS *Majestic* (fifty-six guns), Captain John Hayes

Fifth-rates:
1. HMS *Aeolus* (forty guns), Captain James Townsend
2. HMS *Spartan* (forty-six guns), Captain Edward P. Brenton
3. HMS *Maidstone* (thirty-six guns), Captain George Burdett
4. HMS *Shannon* (thirty-eight guns), Captain Philip Broke

Frigates
1. HMS *Orpheus* (thirty-six guns), Captain Hugh Pigot
2. HMS *Loire* (thirty-eight guns), Captain Blayney
3. HMS *Acasta* (forty guns), Captain Alexander Robert Kerr
4. HMS *Statira* (thirty-eight guns), Captain Hassard Stackpoole
5. HMS *Maidstone* (thirty-six guns), Captain George Burdett
6. HMS *Endymion* (forty-six guns), Captain Henry Hope
7. HMS *Pactolus* (thirty-eight guns), Captain Frederick William Aylmer
8. HMS *Pomone* (thirty-eight guns), Captain Philip Carteret
9. HMS *Narcissus* (thirty-two guns), Captain Alexander Gordon

One of the most famous of British warships, HMS *Victory*, Lord Nelson's flagship at the Battle of Trafalgar. Though it was a 104-gun first-class ship of the line, it closely resembled the configuration of HMS *Superb*. *Courtesy of Thomas Buttersworth.*

Sloops of war
1. HMS *Loup Cervier* (formerly USS *Wasp*, eighteen guns), Commander William Bowen Mends
2. HMS *Atalante* (eighteen guns), Commander Frederick Hickey
3. HMS *Sylph* (eighteen guns), Commander George Dickins
4. HMS *Morgiana* (eighteen guns), Commander David S. Scott

Brig-sloops
1. HMS *Borer* (fourteen guns), Commander Richard Coote
2. HMS *Dispatch* (eighteen guns), Commander James Galloway
3. HMS *Nimrod* (eighteen guns), Lieutenant George Hilton

Bomb ship
1. HMS *Terror* (two mortars), Commander John Sheridan

# A COAST UNDER SIEGE

The *Nimrod* arrived in the waters off Maine after its sea trials in early 1813, when it was attached to the attack squadron of the frigate *Superb*. As had been the case heading off right after its fitting out, the ship wasted no time and went right to work carrying out the designs of Admiral Cochrane. Because the blockade was so effective in cutting off shipping in New England, many towns had little choice but to acquiesce to the demands of the British, simply to survive, in many cases. With the U.S. Navy in little or no position to lift the siege or to effectively engage and destroy the English fleet in detail, coastal towns in the Northeast were left to their own designs to deal with the British as best they could.

Many people on the Cape and islands felt as if the government had abandoned them to the mercy of the enemy, and though it was not an intentional act, the government was, in reality, in no position to offer effective support. In the very simplest terms, these residents were alone. Though a scant comfort, the only saving grace to the people was that the British, owing to their heavy commitments in Europe, were simply unable to send a significant number of troops to support naval operations. In much the same way that the United States had a disproportionate availability of men to ships, so the British had a larger number of ships and fewer men to put ashore. In 1812, the British had about six thousand regulars stationed in and around Canada. And while the militia would bolster these numbers, their contribution was small, as the available population of Canada was only about half a million people, as opposed to the almost eight million citizens of the United States.

The first order of business for the northeast blockade group was to subdue Maine, at the time a part of Massachusetts, allowing it to use the myriad natural harbors as a base of operations in addition to seizing the considerable shipbuilding assets located there. Further, Maine was a key asset in controlling access to the Great Lakes and essentially was the backdoor to England's garrisons in upper and lower Canada. Owing to the number of ships that seemed to appear overnight, and due to their lack of numbers and effective use of available gunboats, Maine was taken with very little fighting and remained under British coastal occupation for the majority of the war.

The British then headed to Cape Cod to establish operations in and around Boston Harbor. Provincetown was taken as a base of operations to survey the harbor and waters north, while below the Cape, the British occupied Naushon Island, employing Tarpaulin Cove, used by American privateers during the Revolution, to keep watch over Buzzards Bay and Block Island, Narragansett Bay and coastal Connecticut, as well as Vineyard and Nantucket Sounds. Being that American gunboats could offer only token resistance to the British, many towns turned to outright bribery to avoid the destruction of their assets. The British could attack coastal towns at will, and their ability to bombard and destroy was greatly feared, as the population had few resources with which to fight back. In fact, if a town did have the resources and were to return fire from coastal installations, as some did, it would only serve to attract more English ships that could moor off the coast and seemingly almost indefinitely lob shells and rockets into the town.

Some towns, such as Brewster and Eastham, which had the majority of their industrial assets right on the shore, paid a ransom to prevent the bombardment of their mills and salt works. Others were less fortunate, such as the residents of Nantucket Island, who were completely cut off. Conditions on the island became so bad that at one point, simply to arrange for food to be brought to the island, they declared themselves neutral, essentially no longer a part of the nation, in order to avoid starvation.

## *NIMROD* JOINS THE FIGHT

It was around this time, in July 1813, that the *Nimrod* was anchored in Tarpaulin Cove, ready to sail at a moment's notice if an American ship was sighted. The ship had seen little action other than assisting in the bombardment of a few towns on the Maine coast since its arrival earlier in the year, and Lieutenant George Hilton, the new master, was eager to prove himself and his command in battle. *Superb* lay anchored off Nantucket, conducting negotiations with the people there to allow limited importation of goods necessary to survival, and so the *Nimrod* was left to its main duties, namely chasing down and destroying any unauthorized merchantmen. On the morning of July 17, 1813, the fifth-rate *Maidstone* was patrolling outside of Tarpaulin Cove when it spotted an American sloop making its way along the shore headed north. It immediately sent up a signal flare and turned about, preparing to give chase to this impetuous American.

The sloop turned out to be the USS *Yorktown*, a twenty-gun privateer under Captain T.W. Story. Since the beginning of the war, it had been very successful operating against British shipping, and the ship and its 140-man crew had taken eleven prizes by mid-1813. As soon as the flare was sighted, the *Nimrod* was a flurry of activity, running up the anchor and unfurling the sails, the crew stowing any unneeded equipment, readying powder and shot for the hungry muzzles of the carronades in the coming engagement. Soon after clearing the cove, the *Nimrod* was joined by the *Poictiers*, a seventy-four-gun third-rate ship of the line well known for the taking or sinking of dozens of merchant and warships since its launch in 1809. For four hours, the *Yorktown* pulled hard on every yard of sail it had, but unfortunately, the same winds from which it derived its speed favored the ship's enemies as well. While it was faster than *Poicters* (though not by much, as it was considered surprisingly speedy for its size), the *Maidstone* and the *Nimrod* were easily the *Yorktown*'s match, and soon it was within range of the *Maidstone*'s rifled guns.

After a few warning shells streaked past the bow that made it apparent what grievous damage they could have caused should they strike home, Captain Story decided that while ignominious, capture was by far the better fate than death, and the *Yorktown* hove to, becoming the *Nimrod*'s first warship captured in American waters. It was not the first vessel to be captured, however. Six days earlier, with the same companions, the *Nimrod* had recaptured the ship *Louisa* and the packet *Manchester*, each of which had, ironically, been captured by the *Yorktown* only weeks earlier. Crewed by unarmed sailors, they surrendered without a shot. After a brief search of the ship, the British sent the *Yorktown* and its crew to the *Halifax*, where they would spend the rest of the war, while the *Yorktown* joined Her Majesty's Royal Navy to be used against its former owners.

Not long after, the *Nimrod* continued its harassment of New England's maritime traders. It drove a ship carrying corn to the people of Nantucket onto the rocks around Woods Hole and, the following month, captured the brig *Anna* out of New Haven. From its base in Tarpaulin Cove, it prowled along the waters of Nantucket Sound to Narragansett Harbor and up the east coast of Cape Cod. The *Manchester* was its next capture, followed by the schooner *Hitta Franklin*. Shortly after December 6, 1813, the *Nimrod* captured the whaling vessel *Chili* loaded with over 1,200 barrels of oil—an extremely valuable commodity, particularly given the naval embargo and the fact that it was used for everything from lubricating the machines necessary for industry to illumination—on the way back to Nantucket after a cruise in the South Seas. And these would only be a few of the merchant vessels it would destroy or capture during the year, certainly earning its nickname as "the scourge of Buzzards Bay."

# Chapter 5

# SAILS, WHALES AND NAILS

## INDUSTRY IN WAREHAM

The Industrious Colonies—The Sacred Cod—Shipbuilding—
Whaling—Iron Manufacturing—Nail Manufacturing—Cotton
Factories—The Burning of the Cotton Factory—King Cranberry

*For want of a nail the shoe was lost; for want of a shoe the horse was lost, and
for want of a horse the rider was lost.*
*—Benjamin Franklin*

Most settlers who arrived in the American colonies in the 1600s were English. The population of the colonies in 1690 was 250,000. By 1790, that number had grown to approximately 2.5 million. During this period, most people were engaged in some form of agriculture. There was a broad agricultural development in the northern colonies of New England (corn, wheat, barley, fruit), whereas the southern colonies relied heavily on the growing of tobacco. Because of the vast untouched resources and its abundant coastline, these early agricultural enterprises quickly gave rise to many other industries, including shipbuilding, iron making and the manufacturing of textiles.

# The Industrious Colonies

Shipbuilding was an industry of primary prominence. The early colonists built wooden ships of varying sizes and weights, ranging from ships of a few hundred tons used primarily for fishing to much larger vessels used in the merchant marine industry, trading with England, other foreign countries and, of course, the West Indies. Towns all along the New England coast— including Boston, Salem, Portsmouth and Wareham—became shipbuilding centers of industry and commerce. The shipbuilding industry gave rise to a multitude of other businesses, including the manufacturing of nails, iron, sails, rope anchors, chains and an assortment of other related enterprises.

The fishing industry in Massachusetts reached its zenith in 1840, with more than 1,300 ships and twelve thousand employees. The largest shipping ports in the state at that time were Boston, New Bedford, Barnstable, Nantucket, Salem, Beverly, Newburyport and Gloucester. The fishing industry prospered in Massachusetts for many years. Coastal fishing and whaling were carried on in most colonies, but in New England, fishing centered on mackerel, bass, herring, halibut, sturgeon and, of course, the famous codfish.

# The Sacred Cod

The Sacred Cod is a four-foot, eleven-inch painted model carved in pine of an Atlantic codfish that has hung in the Massachusetts statehouse in Boston for nearly three hundred years. Reportedly, the first cod symbol was hung in the early Massachusetts House of Assembly in 1729. It was a gift from Judge Samuel Sewall, who had served as a judge during the Salem witch trials, held between February 1692 and May 1693. It was lost in a fire that burned the statehouse in 1747.

A second symbolic carving of the cod appeared sometime between 1748, following the rebuilding of the Massachusetts statehouse, and 1773, when tradesman and painter Thomas Crafts Jr. produced a new replica at the cost of fifteen shillings. The second cod replica was lost during the American Revolution when the British occupied Boston. Speculation remains that the symbolic fish was taken by an unknown British soldier, and it is assumed that it was used as firewood.

The third symbolic cod, the so-named Sacred Cod was hung in the Massachusetts statehouse in 1784, after Boston representative John Rowe requested the legislative chamber "to hang up the representation of a Cod Fish in the room where the House sit, as a memorial of the importance of the Cod-Fishery to the welfare of this Commonwealth." The symbolic fish is suspended above the entrance to the hall in the visitors' gallery. The carved fish remains as an ancient symbol of prosperity for the people in Massachusetts.

A report on the codfish emblem issued in 1895 and compiled by a committee of the Massachusetts House of Representatives declared, "Years before the statesmen of the period had decided to make public acknowledgement of the indebtedness of the colony to the codfish, and had voted to adorn the assembly chamber with a wooden representation thereof, individuals and private corporations were eager to pay tribute to the codfish, and vied with one another in their anxiety to make the recognition as conspicuous as possible."

In 1974, the Massachusetts House voted to make the codfish the official emblem of the state. According to the *Massachusetts Revised Statutes*, Part 1, Title 1, Chapter 2, "The cod shall be the fish or fish emblem and the historic and continuing symbol of the commonwealth."

# SHIPBUILDING

Shipbuilding was one of the oldest industries in the early New England colonies. It swiftly became a profitable industry in Massachusetts because of the colony's miles of coastline with a plethora of safe harbors and bays and its vast supply of raw materials, including a copious number of oak forests. Shipyards in Essex and Suffolk Counties in Massachusetts are recognized for the invention of the traditional American dory and building the famous Gloucester fishing fleet. The dory is a small, shallow boat, about sixteen to twenty-four feet long, lightweight with high sides, a flat bottom and sharp bows. They were easy to build because of their simple lines. For centuries, dories have been used as traditional fishing boats in both coastal waters and the open sea. Early settlements, combined with sawmills, played a major role in the emergence of the shipbuilding industry. A thriving shipbuilding industry began in Massachusetts around 1710.

In the beginning, colonists built their own boats for fishing and transportation. By the late eighteenth century, experienced shipbuilders had begun building a new vessel each winter, fishing it during the summer and selling the vessel during the fall. Wareham, too, was engaged in the shipbuilding business. According Hurd's history of Wareham appearing

Shipbuilding was one of the oldest industries in the early New England colonies because of its miles of coastline and its vast supply of oak forests. The early colonists built wooden ships of varying sizes and weights, including ships of a few hundred tons. *Courtesy of Library of Congress.*

in the 1884 publication, *The History of Plymouth County, Massachusetts: With Biographical Sketches of Many of Its Pioneers and Prominent Men,* "In former years when ship timber was abundant ship building was carried on in this town to a considerable extent. The ships *Pocahontas, Jubilee, Wareham, Kutusoff, George Washington, Republic,* the brig *William Richmond* and a large number of smaller vessels for the coasting trade were built here."

Many of the skills required of shipwrights or shipbuilders were obtained through on-the-job training, and many of the earliest shipyards and boat shops operated as family businesses passed down from generation to generation. A typical shipyard was made up of a lot of land near a bay, inlet, ocean or river way and included a building for yard tools and enough space to store timber. Business was often conducted at the shipbuilder's home. According to historical accounts of the period, "Shipbuilding was an important enterprise in Colonial America and quickly grew into one of the most thriving industries of our young United States. East coast settlements as well as those in Philadelphia and New Hampshire provided protected harbors and bays, small coves and riverbanks, all suitable for construction. Dense forests provided the necessary raw materials."

The need for vessels increased, and soon every seaport on the Atlantic coast was constructing wooden ships. As timber grew scarce in England, it became cheaper to purchase ships built in the colonies. Before the American Revolution, about one-third of the English merchant fleet had been built in America.

The production of these vessels required the skills of various tradesmen and industries, beginning with the shipwright, who drafted the design and directed the craftsmen in their work. Most shipwrights received hands-on training in the family shipyard. Others honed their skills through apprenticeship.

Shipbuilding and design required knowledge of mathematics and geometry because of its endless calculations. A shipwright had to ensure that the ship would float, taking into account the hull's height, weight and volume—no easy undertaking. Although it usually took more than two dozen craftsmen and laborers to ultimately build a seaworthy ship, it was the master shipwright who was in charge of its design and production.

Gangs of laborers known as "saw gangs" were sent to chop down oak and pine timbers to match the measurements of the ship. They cut the wood to precise size and lengths according to the shipwright's design. White pine was used for masts and yellow pine was used for decks because of its resin, which made it more resistant to the sun and saltwater. One of the oldest tools used in building ships was an adze. It was a type of axe with a long blade and bore a slight curve near its handle. Adze men were skilled craftsmen employed in shaping and smoothing the timbers of wood.

The ship's frame was built of hard oak. Carpenters laid the keel, a long, curved beam that ran along the bottom from bow to stern. The ship's ribs were fastened to the keel, completing the boat's framework. The ribs were covered with oak planks, steamed and softened to render them pliable and capable of being curved to fit the shape of the ship. Planks were fastened with wooden pegs called trunnels or tree nails. Some men drilled the holes, while others drove in the trunnels. The planks were then smoothed and planed, and oakum was fed between the planks with a flat-edged caulking iron and mallet. Oakum was a pitch substance consisting of tarred hemp fibers. The seams and cracks around the trunnels were sealed with boiling pine tar to make them watertight. Finally, the hardened surfaces were scraped until smooth.

After the ship was finished and launched, additional artisans and tradesmen were hired to complete the finish work of securing the sails, attaching the anchors and applying all the necessary finishing touches from carving to painting. Whole towns were often engaged in the shipbuilding industry.

# WHALING

By the end of the 1600s, Massachusetts cities and towns—including Plymouth, Salem, Nantucket and much of Cape Cod—were engaged in the whaling industry, supplying sperm oil and whalebone to the colonies and throughout the world. By the early 1700s, New England whaling expanded throughout the world, with perilous journeys extending even to the Arctic waters and Pacific Ocean—wherever whales gravitated.

Sperm oil from a whale's blubber was used for both lighting and lubricating, while the whale bones were used to make a variety of useful

By the early 1700s, New England whaling expanded throughout the world, with perilous journeys extending even to the Arctic waters and Pacific Ocean—wherever whales gravitated. *Courtesy of Library of Congress.*

products including corsets, combs and ornamental jewelry. By the early 1800s, whaling ships from New England were setting out on voyages that could last for years.

Any number of ports in New England sustained the whaling industry, but New Bedford, Massachusetts, became known as the center of the whaling industry. By the 1840s, of the more than seven hundred whaling vessels engaged in the pursuit of their prey on the world's oceans, nearly four hundred of these whaling ships called New Bedford their home port. Wealthy whaling captains built large houses in the best neighborhoods, and New Bedford became known was known as "The City That Lit the World."

The golden age of the New England whaling industry came to an abrupt end in the 1850s with the discovery of oil beneath the ground and the invention of the oil well. The history of the oil business began in 1859 in Pennsylvania when Edwin L. Drake, a career railroad conductor, devised a way to drill a practical oil well. Oil mined from the ground was refined into kerosene for lamps, and the demand for whale oil plunged. Though the whaling industry continued, since whale bone could still be used for a number of household goods, the great American era of the whaling industry disappeared into history.

## IRON MANUFACTURING

Wareham was celebrated for its iron and nail manufactories. Iron making was an industry that reached huge proportions in New England, with Wareham seemingly leading the way. The basic mining and smelting processes generally took place on property where fuel for the ironworks and food for the workers was easy to procure. From the bar iron produced, blacksmiths and other artisans, scattered in villages, towns and cities, fashioned tools, implements and other hardware.

"Among the different manufactures of Wareham that of making cut nails has always held the chief place. Fussing over the feeble attempt to make nails by cutting points and heading them single by hand in a common nail tool the first nailing by machinery was commenced by Isaac and Jared Pratt & Co in the year 1822," wrote the Reverend Noble Warren Everett in his *History of Wareham*, published in 1884.

B. Murdock & Co. built the Washington Iron Works on the Weweantic River in 1822. In 1827, the Poles Works was erected, followed in 1828 by the Tihonet Works and in 1836, the Agawam Works. Besides the manufacture of nails, the town engaged in casting and iron manufacturing. The Franconia Works, located below the Narrows, employed a large number of men making merchantable iron. The first blast furnace was erected in 1805 on the Weweantic River. About 1820, the manufacture of hollow ware, in blast furnaces, was the most thriving business in the area, although most of the furnaces were in Carver and Middleboro. Still, ore ended up in Wareham, where it was hauled to the different furnaces and the manufactured iron products returned to Wareham, where they were shipped.

Whole forests of pitch pine were cut in the iron manufacturing process and converted into coal to fire the furnaces and melt and shape the various iron molds. The introduction of hard coal and pig iron completely revolutionized this business, and blast furnaces were abandoned.

# Nail Manufacturing

The Tremont Nail Company was a nail manufacturing company located in Wareham from 1819 to 2006. It is the oldest manufacturer of steel-cut nails in the country. Making nails for over 180 years, the factory, located at 21 Elm Street, still stands. In the early nineteenth century, Parker Mills was built by shipwrights as a cotton mill. During the War of 1812, it was partially burned by the British. In 1819, another building was constructed on the site by Isaac and Jared Pratt to manufacture nails, and the Parker Mills Nail Company was established. It later became known as the Tremont Nail Company. The first cut nail machines began working in the late 1700s, and the first machine to cut and head a nail in one operation was later invented by Ezekiel Reed of Bridgewater, Massachusetts, in 1786. About 1775, Jeremiah Wilkinson, a Rhode Island inventor, devised a machine that cut nails from a sheet of cold iron. And in 1795, another Massachusetts inventor, Jacob Perkins, patented a nail-making machine that could cut and head nails in a single operation. This machine, which produced up to 200,000 nails per day, made the mass production of nails possible for the first time, and nails became widely available and affordable.

The mill was partially destroyed by fire again in 1836, and reconstruction was completed in 1848. Until the 1920s, the main source of power was a centrifugal water wheel, which powered the massive production. The beams and trusses are mostly wooden-pegged and were built by ship carpenters.

The Tremont Nail Company was a nail manufacturing company located in Wareham, Massachusetts, from 1819 to 2006. It is the oldest manufacturer of steel cut nails in the country. *Courtesy of Library of Congress.*

The bell in the cupola is dated 1851, and its ringing was the audible notice throughout the town to workers over six generations. The main mill is one of five buildings at the site that is over 100 years old. There are also sixty nail machines in the building, many over 125 years old.

Nails in their crudest form date back to 3000 BC. The Romans hand-forged them, and they have been found in excavations and sunken ships from the period AD 500. When the Pilgrims landed in Plymouth, they discovered that the soil was sandy and difficult to cultivate. As they plowed for their first crops, they noticed that the earth yielded small deposits of crude iron ore mixed in with the swampy waters and mud. From this ore and with crude smelters, they separated the metal from the ore and began making nails and metal tools. Cooking utensils, hardware and nails were born out of this muck and mire known as bogs.

## COTTON FACTORIES

The first cotton factory in Wareham was built on the Wankinco River in 1812. This factory was built when spinning cotton in this country was in its earliest stages of development. It was partially burned in 1814 during the *Nimrod* invasion of Wareham. Textile production in the colonies was largely a household business. Imported textiles were expensive, so every home had a spinning wheel and handloom to produce garments and other necessities. Textiles were made chiefly from wool, while cotton was used to a much lesser extent. Before the Revolution, a few shops were established in New England and in other places where several looms were brought together under one roof—a precursor to the cotton manufacturing industry.

In 1812, Curtis Tobey built a cotton factory on a small brook running into the Weweantic River and kept running for several years, but it was not a profitable enterprise and closed. In 1823, Benjamin Lincoln and others built a cotton factory on the Weweantic River where all the improvements in cotton manufacturing were put into place. In 1830, the factory was sold, and the business was carried on for a while by Ezra Thompson & Co. In 1824, Pardon Tabor built a paper mill on the Weweantic River, which ran for many years, and in 1864, Wheelwright & Co. began the manufacture of paper at the former Lincoln cotton mill location.

## THE BURNING OF THE COTTON FACTORY

According to the *History of Plymouth County, Massachusetts: With Biographical Sketches of Many of Its Pioneers and Prominent Men* by D. Hamilton Hurd, published in 1884, when the British invaded Wareham in June 1814, "the enemy then marched up the street stationing sentries upon the high land at convenient distances until they arrived at the cotton factory…they set fire to the shooting a Congreve rocket into a post in the of the first story…The fire was extinguished before it no damage was done."

And according to an account of the cotton mill fire by the Reverend Elias Nason, published in 1890:

> On the 13th of June, 1814, six barges from the British brig-of-war Nimrod *came up to the lower wharf with 220 marines under a flag of truce; seized as prisoners, and hostages for their security, a number of the*

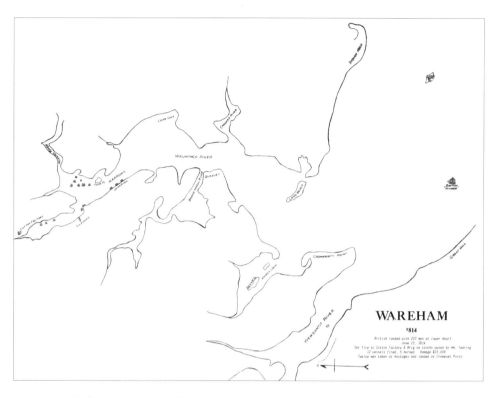

An early line drawing map of Wareham showing the bay and connecting rivers. *Courtesy of Wareham Free Library.*

*inhabitants; fired the Falmouth shipping harbored there; wantonly set fire to the cotton-mill by a rocket; took the powder and ball which the Rev. Noble Everett had brought to the house of Capt. Jeremiah Bumpus; burned a brig on the stocks, and attempted to destroy a ship and brig and five sloops at the wharf; but the fires were soon extinguished.*

# KING CRANBERRY

No historical record of industry in Wareham or, for that matter, Cape Cod would be complete without examining the cranberry business. The American cranberry is one of only three native fruits to North America; blueberries and grapes are the other two. The Native American tribes had a multitude of names for the tart crimson berry. The Leni-Lenape tribe called the cranberry *ibimi*, meaning "bitter berry." They used this wild red berry as a part of their food and as a symbol of peace and friendship. The Chippewas called the cranberry *a'ni-bimin*, the Algonquins called it *atoqua* and the Narragansetts called it *sasemineash*. Native Americans would eat it raw, mixed in with maple sugar, or with deer meat as a pemmican, much like trail mix that could be kept for long periods of time. They also believed that cranberries had medicinal value, and they were used by medicine men as an ingredient in poultices to draw poison from arrow wounds. Cranberry juice was a natural dye for rugs, blankets and clothing.

The colonists named the berry "craneberry" because the flowers looked like the head of the sandhill crane. These birds were observed wading through bogs foraging for cranberries, one of their favorite foods. Over time, the *e* was dropped, and the name was shortened to cranberry. Reportedly, cranberries were offered to the pilgrims at the first Thanksgiving, and during the days of long fishing voyages, barrels of cranberries were kept onboard ships to prevent scurvy.

Cranberries can grow in conditions that would be hostile to most other crops. They grow on low-lying, trailing vines in spongy, waterlogged beds layered with acidic soil, peat, moss, moisture, sand, clay and gravel. These beds are called bogs, and they were formed about ten thousand years ago by glacial deposits.

Although the New England Indian tribes introduced the early settlers to the benefits of cranberries, colonists adapted the crimson berries to their own tastes by creating sauces and breads. They also used them as a preservative. The cranberry was not cultivated until 1816, when Revolutionary captain Henry Hall became the first to successfully cultivate them in Dennis, Massachusetts, on Cape Cod. He discovered that wild cranberries in his bogs were juicier and grew faster after a layer of sand had blown over them. Hall began imitating nature by scattering sand over his cranberry vines and created the cranberry cultivation process that is used to day.

During the 1800s, the number of cranberry growers increased dramatically. By 1885, the industry had expanded from New England into New Jersey, Wisconsin, Oregon, Washington State and Canada. There are two methods for harvesting cranberries: dry harvesting and wet harvesting. The majority of cranberries are harvested using the wet method, which entails flooding bogs with water until the berries float to the surface. Growers then use harvesting machines to loosen the berries from the vine. They are then loaded onto trucks and transported to plants that process them into sauces, juices, jams, jellies, chutneys, relishes, dressings and dried cranberries.

Understanding the role cranberries played in early America is important. The cranberry is one of only a handful of major fruits native to North America. Cranberries were a staple onboard the earliest sailing vessels including whale boats, fishing vessels and war ships. The British sailors used limes to combat scurvy while out on long voyages. American sailors used cranberries for the same thing, as they provided a generous supply of vitamin C, which prevented the illness. Today, Americans consume approximately 400 million pounds of cranberries each year. About 80 million pounds are eaten during Thanksgiving.

# *Chapter 6*
# SUBMISSION—NEVER

Yankee Doodle Topsy-Turvy—The Battle of Hampden—The *Boxer* and the *Enterprise*—New Hampshire Saved from Attack—Little Sister—The Battle of Stonington—Kiss Me Hardy

*Strike now…Chastise the savages for such they are. Make them pay. Our demands may be couched in a single word—Submission.*
—London Times, *August 1814*

The British fleet prowled up and down the New England coast from Maine to Rhode Island, blockading harbors and attacking villages and towns along the way. By the end of 1812, the British had captured Detroit and blockaded South Carolina, Georgia and the Chesapeake and Delaware Bays. By the spring of 1814, the British blockades stretched to the New England coast.

Maine was still a part of Massachusetts during the War of 1812. Because Maine was dependent on the waterways for much of its imports of manufactured goods and the export of their lumber and fish, the blockades were devastating. Many goods and supplies became dangerously scarce, while inflation rose to unprecedented levels. Although the war was initially unpopular in Maine, the blockades and scarcity of goods compelled Mainers to join in the fight. In early September 1813, the British ship *Boxer* and the American vessel *Enterprise* became engaged in a ferocious battle off Mohegan Island. The *Enterprise* was victorious in this raging sea battle.

The British fleet managed to impose its embargo up the entire coast east of Penobscot Bay. President James Madison nationalized the Maine militia and placed it under the control of Major General William King, a local militiaman. The Maine militia, however, had to arm and feed itself, since the federal government had no funds to support it. British landing forces destroyed some crops, and buildings housing stores for winter were burned or destroyed.

# YANKEE DOODLE TOPSY-TURVY

Captain Robert Barrie, a particularly brutal British commander, declared to the citizens in the town of Hampden, Maine, "My business is to burn, sink and destroy. Your town is taken by storm, and by the rules of war, we ought both to lay your village in ashes, and put its inhabitants to the sword. But I will spare your lives, though I mean to burn your houses." His troops sacked the towns of Bangor and Hampden, burning, smashing and looting.

According to *Bangor Daily News* writer Tom Groening, "On a window of a house in Castine, probably sometime in 1814, a British officer took his diamond ring and carved the phrase 'Yankee Doodle Topsy-Turvy,' along with an image of a British flag over an upside-down U.S. flag."

It was, according to Groening, "the equivalent of spitting on the American flag."

"The graffiti merely illustrated the facts—the fledgling United States was, in 1814, under the heel of the British. The empire's troops occupied the town, garrisoned in private homes such as the Whitney house, where the window pane was carved. The house remains on the town's village green, but the window was removed in the early 1980s," Groening wrote.

Another version of this same story appears in Benson J. Lossing's 1869 book, *Pictorial Field Book of the War of 1812*. In it, Lossing writes, "A curious memento of the British at Castine was yet in existence when I visited that place in 1860. It was an outline of the British flag above that of the American flag, and the words 'Yankee Doodle upset,' cut by Lieutenant Elliot, of the British Army, with a diamond on a window-pane in the house of Mrs. Whitney, where some of the officers were quartered. That pane of glass was the only one in the sash at the time of my visit that was not badly cracked."

# The Battle of Hampden

Sir John Sherbrooke led a British force, including a British squadron from the Royal Navy base at Halifax, to capture the coastal Maine town of Machias in August 1814. Sherbrooke's forces included the warships HMS *Dragon*, HMS *Endymion*, HMS *Bacchante*, HMS *Sylph* and a contingency of some three thousand British troops. The goal of the British was to reestablish British title to Maine east of the Penobscot River, an area the British had renamed "New Ireland," and open the line of communications between Halifax and Quebec.

Along the way, Sherbrooke learned that the USS *Adams* was under repair at Hampden, on the Penobscot River. He subsequently changed his plan of attack and headed straight for Castine, located at the mouth of the Penobscot River. He joined forces with four more Bristish ships, the HMS *Bulwark*, HMS *Tenedos*, HMS *Peruvian* and the schooner HMS *Pictou*. When the huge British fleet sailed into the Castine cove, the local Maine militia fled, leaving the town unprotected.

Sherbrooke told the inhabitants that if they went about their business as usual, kept out of the way and surrendered their weapons, they would be protected as British subjects. He also claimed that his forces would pay fair prices for all goods and services provided. The inhabitants did not challenge the occupation, although more than one thousand militiamen organized just outside Belfast.

On September 2, Captain Robert Barrie landed with his troops three miles below Hampden and waited. The next day, September 3, the British troops moved on Hampden, led by Lieutenant Colonel Henry John, and were met with some resistance at Pitcher's Brook, but this was short-lived. The prospect of the well-organized British troops converging on them caused the militia to break ranks and flee, heading toward Bangor. Before the British troops could capture the USS *Adams*, the ship was blown up.

At this point, Captain Barrie ordered two hundred men to take control of Hampden while he and the balance of his force pursued the militia in the direction of Bangor. Eighty prominent men of the Hampden area spent a night as prisoners. Most were paroled the next day. Supported by three of his ships, Barrie entered an intimidated Bangor at midday and called for unconditional submission. Provisions and quarters were demanded. Although Barrie ordered a ban on liquor for his troops, some men managed to acquire brandy by the bucket. Barrie then ordered all the liquor in the town to be destroyed. This set off a wave of plundering. Six stores fell to the mob, and $6,000 worth of property was damaged. Many citizens fled the town.

During the night, the British burned fourteen vessels across the river, but before the British troops could burn Bangor ships, the town's selectmen made a deal. They offered Barrie a $30,000 bond and agreed to complete four ships on the stocks and deliver them to him in Castine. Barrie accepted the arrangement and carried away a packet, four schooners and a boat. Bangor selectmen estimated that the losses and damages totaled approximately $45,000.

The Bangor incident did not end the troubles for Hampden. Barrie decided to spend more time there, and his troops terrorized the town, killing livestock and destroying homes. Two ships moored off the town were burned. The rampage prompted a town committee to appeal to Barrie to treat the place with a little humanity. His shocking reply summarized his approach. Barrie did not follow through on his threat to burn down Hampden houses, but he did get a $14,000 bond on several incomplete vessels. The terms of the agreement with Barrie required the completed vessels be delivered to the Royal Navy in Castine by November 1. The Battle of Hampden ended in complete victory for the British troops.

On June 16, the HMS *Bulwark*, carrying about ninety guns, anchored off the mouth of Saco River in Maine. The ship's commander sent 150 armed men, in five large boats, to destroy property of Thomas Cutts. Cutts met the invading troops waving a white flag. He proposed paying the troops in lieu of destroying his property. Despite Cutt's pleas, the troops were ordered to burn Cutt's two ships and plundered his store of goods.

Sherbrooke declared the region "New Ireland" and a province of British-controlled Canada. With the signing of the Treaty of Ghent in December 1814, the British claim to Maine was ended. The British evacuated Castine in April 1815. Ironically, the most important result of the War of 1812 on Maine was that it propelled the movement for independence from Massachusetts. The failure of Massachusetts to help Maine during the British invasion brought the matter to a head. William King, who had been in charge of the Maine militia, became the leader for the drive for a separate Maine statehood. Maine achieved statehood in 1820, and King was elected the state's first governor.

## THE *BOXER* AND THE *ENTERPRISE*

On September 5, 1813, the USS *Enterprise* sighted the HMS *Boxer* off the coast of Pemaquid Point, Maine. The *Enterprise* had fourteen eighteen-pound cannons on board and a crew of 102 men. The *Boxer* had twelve cannons and a crew of 66 men. The *Enterprise* was under the command of U.S. Navy lieutenant William Ward Burrows. A British vessel, the *Boxer* was under the control of Commander Samuel Blyth.

Blyth prepared for battle by nailing his ship's flag to the foremast, a time-honored defiant naval signal demonstrating the refusal to surrender and the willingness to fight to the last man. Not to be outdone symbolically, Burrows positioned one of his cannons on the stern of his ship, proclaiming, "We are going to fight both ends and both sides of this ship as long as the ends and the sides hold together."

When the two ships opened fire on each other, Blyth was killed immediately in the fusillade. Burrows met a similar fate shortly afterward, dying on board the *Enterprise*. The ferocious sea battle lasted approximately thirty minutes and ended with the HMS *Boxer* all but destroyed. The *Enterprise* headed into port in Portland with the captured *Boxer* in tow. The Maine sea battle gained international attention because both commanding officers, the *Boxer*'s Samuel Blyth and the *Enterprise*'s William Burrows, were killed in action. The dying Burrows declined to accept Blyth's sword, directing it be sent to the family of the dead British captain.

"I am satisfied. I die contented," Burrows reportedly proclaimed on his deathbed. Both commanders were given elaborate funerals and laid to rest side by side in Portland's Eastern Cemetery. Blyth and Burrows were buried with full military honors, and a tombstone was placed over their graves. Blyth was twenty-nine years old. Burrows was twenty-eight.

On September 5, 1813, the USS *Enterprise* sighted the HMS *Boxer* off the coast of Pemaquid Point, Maine. The ferocious sea battle lasted approximately thirty minutes and ended with the HMS *Boxer* all but destroyed. *Courtesy Library of Congress.*

## NEW HAMPSHIRE SAVED FROM ATTACK

The navy yard and the forts in Portsmouth Harbor were early exposed to the British naval onslaught against the New England coast. The entire New Hampshire coastline was in anger. British ships were prowling the coast and, in one incident, entered the Bay of the Piscataqua River, a twelve-mile river that runs southeast and defines a portion of the border between New Hampshire and Maine. It empties into Portsmouth Harbor.

On the night of June 21, it was reported that the British were landing troops at Rye, intent on attacking Portsmouth. It proved to be a false alarm, but still, the strong military defenses at Portsmouth kept the port from British attack. In early September, the entire New Hampshire militia was ordered on alert, ready to march to defend Portsmouth.

The New Hampshire militia manned the Portsmouth forts, and still others were placed along the surrounding hills and plains to guard against an attack from forces landing at Hampton or Rye. When the British forces learned of the militia's defense of the port, they decided against attacking and withdrew their vessels. According to one report provided by a British spy who reconnoitered just outside Portsmouth, "The town was swarming with soldiers, and well-defended." New Hampshire was saved from attack.

## LITTLE SISTER

The most dramatic battle along the New England coast was the defeat of British forces at Stonington, Connecticut. The attack lasted three days, August 9–12, 1814. The British forces were led by the famous British naval hero Captain Thomas Hardy. It was Hardy who, in 1830, was appointed first naval lord, the professional head of the Royal Navy, and who served with Admiral Lord Horatio Nelson during most of Nelson's great naval victories during the Napoleonic Wars (1803–1815). Hardy was with Nelson when Nelson was killed during the Battle of Trafalgar in 1805. Despite his many victories and seafaring acumen, his attack on Stonington was a major defeat for him.

Hardy had a squadron of about 1,500 men. The defenders of Stonington numbered approximately 20 men and only two cannons. A group of five British warships anchored off Stonington and shelled the city. The British forces fired approximately fifty tons of cannon fire on the town during the attack, setting forty buildings on fire while only managing to kill one horse and a goose. Reports indicate that the British forces lost 21 men killed and 50 more wounded. When word of the defeat spread, the loss by Hardy and his British forces caused great exhilaration throughout the country, as well as embarrassment to the British command. The victory at Stonington so bedeviled Hardy's forces that further attempts to capture or destroy Connecticut seaports were abandoned.

Stonington honors this defense of the town during this attack with a granite monument. In 1830, an obelisk, topped with a naval shell, was erected in Stonington's Cannon Square. The inscription on the monument reads, "These two guns of 18 pounds caliber were heroically used to repel the attack on Stonington of the English naval vessels *Ramillies*, 74 guns, *Pactolus*, 44, *Dispatch*, 20, *Nimrod*, 20 and the bomb ship *Terror*. August 10, 1814."

A further inscription on the monument has the Latin motto "*In perpetuamrei memoriam*," meaning "In everlasting remembrance of the event." The monument also includes the list of names of the town's defenders who manned the cannons during the attack. The names include:

> *THE DEFENDERS OF THE FORT*
> *AUG. 10, 1814*
> *GEO. HOWE FELLOWES*
> *WHO NAILED THE FLAG TO THE MAST*
> *AMOS DENISON, JR.*
> *JERE. HALEY*
> *SIMEON HALEY*
> *JERE. HOLMES*
> *SETH C. LEONARD*
> *ASA LEE*
> *THOS. WILCOX*
> *WILLIAM POTTER*
> *HORATIO G. LEWIS*

The two cannons used by Stonington defenders flank the monument. Several of the British shells that tore through village homes and set them ablaze now sit atop small granite pedestals in front of a home on Main Street and in front of the Stonington Free Library.

While the battle was not strategically important, from an emotional and psychological standpoint, it was vital, according to local author James de Kay, author of *The Battle of Stonington: Torpedoes, Submarines and Rockets*

The Stonington Battle Flag is considered by some to be the "little sister" of the "Star-Spangled Banner" since each survived a British attack within just weeks of the other. *Courtesy of Library of Congress.*

*in the War of 1812.* According to De Kay, "America at the time was having trouble with the war. Things were not going well but suddenly this tiny little town of Stonington was victorious and sent the British Navy away with its tail between its legs. For a couple or three weeks, Stonington was the biggest news in America." De Kay said that Hardy and the British had made a mistake in underestimating the tenacity of the people of Stonington.

The most prized artifact of the attack is the sixteen-stars-and-stripes flag that the defenders flew during the battle. It is kept in a climate-controlled room at the Stonington Historical Society after being displayed for years in Stonington's Cannon Square. On August 10, during a lull in the attack, Stonington defenders nailed a large American flag to a pole above their cannon battery. It was a banner of defiance that waved until the British sailed away on the afternoon of August 12, similar to the now famous, "Star-Spangled Banner" flag, which flew over Fort McHenry when a British fleet of nineteen ships attacked the Baltimore fort on September 12, 1814. And like the "Star-Spangled Banner," the Stonington flag withstood the bombardment as a testament to the American resolve in times of war.

Fort McHenry withstood continuous British shelling for twenty-five hours in heavy rain. When the British ships were unable to pass the fort and penetrate the harbor, the attack was ended, and on the morning of September 14, when the battered flag still flew above the ramparts, it was clear that Fort McHenry remained in American hands. This revelation was famously captured in poetry by Francis Scott Key, an American lawyer and amateur poet. He composed a poem originally titled "Defense of Fort. McHenry," which was later put to the music of a common tune and retitled "The Star-Spangled Banner." It was adopted as the United States national anthem by a congressional resolution on March 3, 1931.

Francis Scott Key, an American lawyer and amateur poet composed a poem originally titled "Defense of Fort McHenry," which was later put to the music of a common tune and retitled the "Star-Spangled Banner." *Courtesy Library of Congress.*

The Stonington Battle Flag is considered by some to be the "little sister" of the "Star-Spangled Banner" since each survived a British attack within just weeks of the other. Stonington's flag of loosely woven wool bunting was sewn for the local militia, the Eighth Company of the Thirtieth Connecticut Regiment. It was big, approximately twelve feet by eighteen feet.

## THE BATTLE OF STONINGTON

Captain Hardy, in command of the attacking British fleet, had been given orders to attack towns along the New England coast. For unknown reasons, Hardy decided not to attack the Connecticut towns of New London, Mystic or Saybrook. Stonington, therefore, became his prime target. On August 9, 1814, four British ships were under Hardy's command, including the

*Ramillies*, the *Pactolus*, the bomb ship *Terror* and the brig *Dispatch*. He anchored his fleet within two miles of the town and then sent a flag of truce ashore with the following message to the Stonington authorities: "Not wishing to destroy the unoffending inhabitants residing in the town of Stonington, one hour is granted them from the receipt of this to remove out of the town." In answer to a question whether it was Hardy's intention to destroy the town, the Stonington authorities were assured that it was. The Stonington authorities sent Hardy the following response: "We shall defend the place to the last extremity; should it be destroyed, we will perish in its ruins!"

The residents agreed they would fight, and the British rowboat carried the message back to Hardy. The sick, infirmed, women, children and those unable to fight left the town, and the inhabitants' most valuable possessions were taken away or hidden. A few Stonington militiamen were stationed on the point of the narrow peninsula on which Stonington stands to guard against a possible landing attempt by the British forces.

Two old cannons had been hidden away and were subsequently called into action to defend the town. Hardy did not know the Stonington militia still had the two cannons hidden away in a shed near what is now the Stonington Free Library. They were hauled to a small fort overlooking the harbor where the British fleet was anchored, and the two cannons, as well as a smaller one, were eventually used to great success in inflicting a great deal of damage to the invading forces. Also working in the militia's favor was the appearance of Jeremiah Holmes, who had been forced into service by the Royal Navy for three years before he escaped. While with the British, he became an expert marksman with a cannon. Holmes was now given the opportunity to use his skills against his former oppressors, and he used them well.

The bomb ship *Terror* began firing incendiary shells on the village. It also fired rockets and cannonballs that tore through wooden structures. Over the next three days, the Americans fired the two cannons at the enemy, nearly destroying the British vessel *Dispatch*, which was about a quarter mile offshore. Another of the ships, the frigate *Pactolus*, got stuck in shallow water off Sandy Point and had to unload cannonballs and shot in order to float free. Residents later salvaged the pieces. The largest of the warships, the seventy-four-gun *Ramillies*, was anchored two miles off shore and out of range of the American cannons. The two sides intermittently fired back and forth with periods of heavy bombardment by the British. Two British sailors were killed, and more were wounded. One Stonington militiaman died several weeks later from complications from an injury he suffered in the battle. The shells from the *Terror* discharged a trail of flaming cannon fire

Captain Thomas Hardy, in command of the attacking British fleet, had been given orders to attack towns along the New England coast. *Courtesy National Maritime Museum.*

that ignited buildings on shore. The fires were quickly extinguished by fire crews. While about half of the 120 structures in the borough were hit, only about 15 sustained serious damage. None were destroyed.

The bombardment back and forth kept up through the night and into the day. During a brief cease-fire, the British forces determined that no life had been lost and no serious damage inflicted on the shore. Holmes, the cannon marksman extraordinaire, had kept the militia battery of two old iron cannon busy. Finally, Holmes's ammunition gave out, and a search of the town turned up no more powder or ammunition. Luckily, this remained unknown to the British forces. Stonington was defenseless and at the mercy of the invaders. Several residents suggested that they propose a formal surrender by lowering the flag that was floating high over their heads. Holmes indignantly refused to surrender. "No!" he told the crowd. "That flag shall never come down while I am alive!" And it didn't.

Unknown to the Stonington defenders, Hardy had already given orders to cease the bombardment and retreat from the harbor. The *Ramillies* and *Pactolus* fired three final blasts at the town, which were merely a parting

King George III (1738–1820) was only nominally the head of the British state. Nicknamed "mad King George," it was well known that he suffered from mental problems and real governmental power lay in the hands of regents and the prime minister.

salute. Hardy's ships withdrew, although the *Terror* kept up a bombardment for several hours as Hardy's fleet sailed out of the harbor. Stonington had been saved. The victory prompted poet Philip Freneau to write the poem, "The Battle of Stonington, on the Seaboard of Connecticut," which reads, in part:

> *Four gallant ships from England came*
> *Freighted deep with fire and flame,*
> *And other things we need not name,*
> *To have a dash at Stonington.*
> *Now safely moor'd, their work begun,*
> *They thought to make the Yankees run,*
> *And have a mighty deal of fun*
> *In stealing sheep at Stonington.*
> *They kill'd a goose, they kill'd a hen,*
> *Three hogs they wounded in a pen—*
> *They dash'd away,—and pray what then?*
> *This was not taking Stonington.*
> *To have their turn, they thought but fair;*
> *The Yankees brought two guns to bear,*
> *And, sir, it would have made you stare,*

*This smoke of smokes at Stonington.*
*They bor'd* Pactolus *through and through,*
*And kill'd and wounded of her crew*
*So many, that she bade adieu*
*To the gallant boys of Stonington.*
*The brig* Despatch [sic] *was hull'd and torn—*
*So crippled, riddled, so forlorn—*
*No more she cast an eye of scorn*
*On the little fort at Stonington.*
*The* Ramillies *gave up th' affray,*
*And, with her comrades sneaked away.*
*Such was the valor on that day,*
*Of British tars, near Stonington.*
*But some assert, on certain grounds,*
*(Besides the damage and the wounds,)*
*It cost the King ten thousand pounds*
*To have a dash at Stonington.*

# KISS ME HARDY

Lord Admiral Horatio Nelson (September 29, 1758–October 21, 1805) was a British naval commander, famous for his service during the Napoleonic Wars. He was wounded several times in combat, losing one arm in battle. His most famous was the Battle of Trafalgar in 1805, during which he was shot and killed. He was hit by a musket ball fired from a French ship and died below decks. His body was preserved in a barrel of brandy.

His second in command was Thomas Hardy, who had been defeated in his attempt to attack Stonington. Hardy was with Nelson when the admiral was shot and killed. According to historical accounts, on his deathbed, Nelson asked Hardy to kiss him before he died, mouthing the words, "Kiss me, Hardy." According to the contemporary accounts, Nelson last words were: "Take care of my dear Lady Hamilton, Hardy, take care of poor Lady Hamilton." He paused then said very faintly, "Kiss me, Hardy." Hardy kissed him on the cheek. Nelson then said, "Now I am satisfied. Thank God I have done my duty." Then Nelson died.

# Chapter 7
## ON TO WAREHAM

CHANGE OF TACTICS—ALL WAR IS TERRIBLE—UNTO THE BREECH—BEST
LAID PLANS—DEMANDS NOT MET—ON TO WAREHAM—PASSED OVER ONCE

*South of the Cape HMS* Nimrod *ruled the waters of Nantucket and Vineyard
Sounds and Buzzard's Bay. These vessels captured and often ransomed such
coasting and fishing vessels as ventured out. Their armed barges made frequent
forays and landings on the coast to destroy shipping and obtain fresh provisions.*
—*Samuel Eliot Morison,* The Maritime History of Massachusetts,
1783–1860, *1922*

By 1814, British tactics began to take a new turn owing to the stalemate
the war had reached in its second year. Given the lack of U.S. sea power
and the English inability to reinforce its troops on land, neither side was
in any position to provide a decisive victory, despite the ongoing loss of
ships, materiel and lives, with neither a foreseeable end nor gain of riches or
territory in the near future. A major turn of events would shift the situation
into England's favor, however. In 1814, Napoleon had been defeated and
forced to abdicate the throne of France, thus beginning his exile to the island
of Elba. The British government was growing weary of the war, and now that
Napoleon was (for the time being) no longer a threat, it had the means to shift
a significant amount of military resources to North America and accordingly
had made plans to effect a decisive victory by making a thrust by land and by
sea across the eastern seaboard. Though the attacking of civilians and private

Napoleon Bonaparte (1769–1821), French general, later emperor and perhaps one of the greatest military tacticians of all time. *Courtesy Library of Congress.*

property were by no means a new concept in warfare, British tactics were taking an increasing turn toward the punitive destruction of nonmilitary targets.

## CHANGE OF TACTICS

Until early 1814, English tactics had hinged on a water-based strategy, taking or destroying American shipping and goods, while they largely ignored attacking land-based targets or property necessary to the survival of noncombatant civilians. Partly, this was due to the aforementioned lack of soldiery available to the British, and while higher notions of decency didn't factor prominently in the decision to leave civilians unmolested, it was in essence a simple lack of necessity. At best, maiming or killing non-soldiers won the British no tactical or strategic military advantage, and at worst, it could bring unwanted political headaches. Until now, the British, though at war with the Americans, had still enjoyed some measure of trade and even support from the populace in that they could fairly easily procure supplies and intelligence, if not through trade, then with a minimum of necessary violence. Beyond this, a basic fact of war is that atrocity breeds atrocity—or as the German saying goes, "revenge seldom goes long unrevenged."

## ALL WAR IS TERRIBLE

All war is, of course, terrible, but one must nonetheless weigh all costs versus benefits of every action in such dreadful endeavors, as once the human fuse of brutality and viciousness is lit, the cost can quite rapidly turn any conflict

The British army preferred to fight in organized lines, as they did portrayed here at Bunker Hill. There was a strong resentment toward Americans on the part of the English, who felt that firing from concealed positions was contrary to the honorable approach to fighting a war. *Courtesy of Library of Congress.*

into a pyrrhic victory. Indeed, in the Revolution, Americans had shown themselves more than willing to employ whatever tactics required to harass, demoralize or destroy the British, and perhaps nothing more offended their sense of "fair play" than being fired on from concealed positions, having pot-shots taken at them or being shot at from behind. And while the British had years of experience fighting adversaries in North America who employed these tactics well before the War of 1812 began—first against the natives, then the French and finally their own former countrymen—they still preferred battles that were fought on open ground according to established rules of war. The Americans, because they were badly outnumbered, outgunned, inexperienced and ill equipped, used guerrilla-type tactics.

Now, British tactics were to take a turn from a defensive operation—holding back the United States from Canada and the Great Lakes—to an offensive one, with a clear notion of what they wished to achieve. According to George Daughan in his book *1812: The Navy's War*, he asserts that the British hoped to realize seven strategic points that would have dramatically altered the makeup of the United States, if not eliminated it as a viable country altogether (thus potentially bringing it, even if partially, back under English control). They were:

1. Expulsion of the United States from French territory gained in the Louisiana Purchase, as well as from Spanish Florida.

2. British control of the Oregon Territory.
3. British control of the Mississippi River.
4. British control of Great Lakes.
5. Establishment of Indian reserves and a buffer zone between the United States and Canada in the area bounded by Great Lakes, the Ohio River and the Mississippi River.
6. Separation of the already antiwar New England states from United States as initial step to incorporating them into Canada.
7. Dissolution of U.S. rights to fish in the waters around Newfoundland, which had been granted under the 1783 Treaty of Paris, essentially destroying the cornerstone of New England's economy.

From the view of the beleaguered citizens of New England, these aims must have seemed well within Britain's grasp, and unless there was a drastic turn of events in favor of the Americans, one couldn't blame the citizens of southeastern Massachusetts for thinking that the Crown was about to make a return.

## UNTO THE BREECH

On January 28, 1814, Admiral Cochrane determined that lighting the fuse that could lead to the final conflagration was a risk worth taking. Earlier in the month, an innkeeper named Slocum reportedly overheard a group of British naval officers discussing a plan to attack Falmouth. Ironically, Slocum's inn was located in none other than Tarpaulin Cove. The cove served as the British base of operations for their depredations against southeastern Massachusetts for what oftentimes turns out to be the best reason for choosing any site for extended tactical operations, particularly against a static enemy: geography.

Tarpaulin Cove lies on the southern side of Naushon Island in what is now Gosnold, Massachusetts. Though it had been inhabited by the British (and later Americans) since the 1600s, a lighthouse and inn had been built there in 1759 by one Zaccheus Lumbert. His establishment was meant to provide food, rest and comfort to whalers and the coastal traders and sailors common in the region. The inn and lighthouse fell into some disrepair by the turn of the century, and in another twist of irony, the government had decided in 1807 to establish funds for a new lighthouse, which would have meant there was more of a government presence there.

Then as now, however, the government was slow in procuring funds, and the light had not been built by the time Captain Newton decided to make it his center of command. Having been a favorite bay for whalers and fishermen, it also had a long history as a haven for pirates and privateers alike. Tarpaulin Cove, lies, as said, in a most strategically advantageous position at the head of Buzzard's Bay off Massachusetts's southern coast, just north of Martha's Vineyard and within striking distance of Block Island and its sound, Narragansett Bay, Mount Hope Bay, Long Island Sound and the entire coastline of Connecticut. While many towns, large and small—such as New Bedford, Fairhaven, Pocasset, Wareham, Mattapoisett and Falmouth—were tempting targets, it was Falmouth that drew the unfortunate choice as a first strike for Britain.

## Best Laid Plans

The town had been an ongoing nuisance to Britain's fleet, taking great pride in tricking Cochrane's ships into going out on wild goose chases, sowing false rumors or by stealing back prize vessels (usually small fishing craft) that had been taken. Further, the residents flaunted the inability of the British to land there, the militia, under Captain Weston Jenkins (who would go on later in the war to capture a British sloop of war in dramatic games of cat and mouse), being a very visible presence that were dug in and prepared to defend the town at a moment's notice, any time of day or night. Apparently, the officers had plans to make a landing in Falmouth in order to seize two brass cannon that had been prominently displayed and fired, though to this point without inflicting any damage on approaching ships, as well as a small sloop from Nantucket, which, due to its status as an occupied island, the British felt was public property that had been captured as a legitimate war prize.

The important distinction here is that the British navy tended to focus on the seizure or destruction of what was considered "public property"—namely guns, powder, cannon, ships and any other supplies the Americans could use in military operations. In time, this definition became so broad as to include food; factories of a distinctly nonmilitary nature, such as textile mills; and fishing boats. Eventually, the pretext was dropped when Admiral Cochrane simply ordered the wholesale destruction of any coastal communities. There were particularly hard feelings toward the communities of southeastern Massachusetts, and so the officers felt that Falmouth was a good start.

# DEMANDS NOT MET

When the *Nimrod* arrived at 10:00 a.m. on January 28, it immediately sent ashore a barge under a flag of truce to discuss the crew's intentions. Being that it was a hazy morning, the approach of the barges had gone undetected until it was too late for the militia to assemble in force at the beach to meet with or—if need be—drive off the invaders. As it was, crew members encountered only a small picket party. Once ashore, they demanded a meeting with the commanding officer in the area, delivering their ultimatum to Captain Jenkins: that the "two brass cannon and the Nantucket sloop be handed over, or the *Nimrod* would commence bombardment of the town." In order to escape the attention of the British, many towns, if they possessed field pieces, would frequently attempt to dismantle and hide them in such a way that they could be quickly retrieved and assembled for action. If the ruse worked, the town would usually be ignored or, at most receive, a hasty examination by a landing party.

Owing to the fact that they could rapidly find themselves heavily outnumbered if the militia had time to assemble, landing parties tended to have specific agendas they could carry out quickly. According to local legend, the ever-defiant Jenkins told the British party, "If you want our cannon, you can come and get them, and we will give you what's in them first." (What he literally said, however, was that the British could come and get them if they wanted them, which the English officers interpreted as a challenge.) The barges returned to *Nimrod,* and Captain Jenkins made preparations to evacuate what they could from the town, moving the sick and infirm, women and children, along with furniture and anything else they could possibly save from the inevitable attack to come, as Lieutenant Hilton made it clear he would commence his bombardment at noon if the demands were not met.

True to his word, at about noon, *Nimrod* commenced firing broadsides into the town, targeting any building in range, paying particular attention to high-value targets, namely saltworks, mills and factories. This fire was kept up through the day until nightfall. They had severely damaged some thirty houses and all but destroyed the saltworks and set alight several smaller buildings, but despite their furious bombardment, the British were unable to land at Falmouth and were forced to retire—without the sloop or the cannons of which they had come to take possession.

# On to Wareham

After the failure of the attack on Falmouth, the British set their hand to terrorizing other targets, and so *Nimrod* continued to hover outside the bays of New Bedford and Fairhaven, restricting shipping but unable to strike, owing to the guns of Fort Phoenix and other batteries ringing Clark's Cove and the militia amassed in the surrounding area (though the batteries weren't of any great number at one single time).

By June 1814, however, *Nimrod* was fully back in action and systematically preying on the towns of southeastern Massachusetts. While some towns paid a ransom to avoid British depredations, others could or would not do so, often at their own peril. The town of Brewster had been threatened with bombardment if it failed to provide salt for the British, and many towns along the southern shore of Cape Cod suffered from similar blackmail throughout the war. Indeed, the entire Cape remained on edge.

Being effectively bottled up by the British base in Provincetown, Plymouth sent out calls to the Duxbury and Kingstown militias for assistance in guarding its harbor from a landing by royal marines. Their fears were fueled in part by recent action off Scituate in which the heavy frigate USS *Chesapeake*, departing Boston under a white flag bearing the inscription "Free Trade and Sailor's Rights," encountered and was engaged by the HMS *Shannon*, whose captain had—in the local newspaper, no less—for all intents and purposes baited the captain of the Chesapeake into a single ship-to-ship contest. (Many historians discount this as having had any effect on the captain's decision to meet the *Shannon*, however, as he had made clear prior to its publication that he intended to sail in any case.)

Twenty miles off the coast of Boston, the two vessels met and began a furious exchange of broadsides. The ships would maneuver close to each other until they were close enough that the crews began making attempts to board each. The ensuing carnage—in which Captain James Lawrence uttered the now famous words "Don't give up the ship" after he was mortally wounded by a sniper—took only fifteen minutes from beginning to end.

Only a few days later, royal marines from the HMS *Nymph* landed at Scituate, tasked with destroying any ship they found in the harbor. Ten vessels, mainly small fishing and coastal traders, were burned, and the point was made: any town on the coast could be next. There was enough militia in the area to protect the towns, but the trouble was that they were poorly organized and inefficiently led.

View of the bay looking out from one of the gun emplacements of Fort Phoenix. Built to take advantage of the natural rock formations and height above the water, the formidable edifice could rain destruction on any position in the Fairhaven-New Bedford harbor. *Courtesy Schlitzer90 (own work) [CC-BY-SA-3.0 (http://creativecommons. org/licenses/by-sa/3.0)], via Wikimedia Commons.*

*Shannon* fires on *Chesapeake*. Captain Broke was known as a master gunner who not only made significant improvements to how guns were sighted but also drilled his men hard in their efficient use. This expertise was evident in the fact that during the engagement, *Shannon* was hit 158 times, while *Chesapeake* was struck by 362 projectiles. *Courtesy Library of Congress.*

Captain James Lawrence (1781–1813) was the commanding officer of USS *Chesapeake*. Mortally wounded by a sniper during the action, he is well known for his dying command: "Don't give up the ship."*Courtesy of Yale University Art Gallery.*

Worse, political opinions on how the war should be conducted differed widely from one town to the next. While Plymouth received the help it requested in troop strength, when Cohasset asked the government of the commonwealth for two cannon with which to protect its harbor, not only was the request denied, but it was also suggested the town instead raise a white flag and hope the British would show mercy. Luckily, however, when it was learned that there was an intended English attack converging on Cohasset, militia and artillery companies from Hingham, Weymouth, Hanover, Randolph and other neighboring communities began to amass and prepare to make a defense of the town. When the expected force of Royal Navy barges and men arrived, a reconnoitering force of officers decided that an attack was ill advised, as the town "presented the appearance of a military camp" and decided withdrawal was the better option before them.

## PASSED OVER ONCE

During the Revolution, as well as in the current conflict, Wareham had been passed over by the British, despite being a known haven for privateers. The town, however, had thus far escaped attack by attempting to appear as loudly neutral as possible, a typical New England town going about its business, offending no one. At the turn of the century, Wareham had become a very prosperous manufacturing town, being known for its iron works, cotton mill, leather tanning and thriving shipbuilding industry.

While the town adhered to the letter of the law regarding the raising and maintenance of a militia, there were many who felt that the appearance of soldiers necessarily implied martial intent—that by having them visible, they would attract the very people they wanted to stay away, just as keeping them clandestine would have the opposite effect and keep them from attracting their attention in the first place. Indeed, the town was familiar with how to keep resistance activity under wraps. Captain John Kendrick was a prominent resident of Wareham and commander of the sloop *Fanny*. Colonel David Nye, who had been present at Falmouth as well as the commander of the local militia regiment, was also master of the *Sea Flower*, a privateer that had been fitted out for combat in Wareham, as had the ten-gun sloop *Hancock*. Wareham was without any artillery, though it did have several dozen militia in town and was able to call on more if needed, though in this war, the British used hit-and-run tactics, bombarding settlements, burning wharves and docks and then disappearing just as quickly, melting away into the blackness of the Atlantic.

Wareham is located at the very head of Buzzards Bay, with many small inlets such as Wings Cove and Sedge Cove to the south, and is bordered on the east by the Weweantic River. Though the town has much coastline, the water is not particularly deep. Thus, larger ships of the line could not get to any closer than within five or six miles of the coast, where they could not do much damage. Smaller vessels, such as *Nimrod*, could get heavy guns fairly close to shore but were more easily spotted. For this, the ever-inventive British had another type of vessel: the barge. The most effective British patrol vessels were the barges carried by the warships. The second-largest of a warship's boats, a barge was usually thirty-six feet long and was propelled by either sails from its single mast or twelve oars. Armed with muskets, cutlasses and sometimes a swivel gun and large enough to carry a complement of royal marines, a barge could threaten lightly defended shore installations or overtake and capture coasting vessels in the sound. And it would be these very vessels that were headed for Wareham.

# Chapter 8

# THE ATTACK

*Let's think of our heroes, our men of renown*
*The battles they fought, the victories they won;*
*And praise our brave heroes of valorous deed,*
*Who deserve well of us our tribute of need.*
*—Nathaniel Coverly, "Peace, Peace," 1815*

It was the dead of night on June 12, 1814, when the third-rate ship of the line *Superb*, accompanied by the *Nimrod*, made its way out of Tarpaulin Cove and headed north-northwest once again toward the mouth of the Acushnet River and New Bedford Harbor. Standing nearby was another seventy-four-gun third-rate, HMS *La Hogue*, which had joined *Superb*'s group in pursuing privateers (they had chased the schooner *Yankee* on its way into port and were now watching intently) and blockading New Bedford Harbor.

## A Final Stab at an Old Foe

Though they had certainly been busy with other pursuits, Captains Paget and Newton had spent the better part of the past two years harassing, shadowing and otherwise attempting to destroy the ability of the two towns to conduct any sort of maritime activity. And while they had enjoyed some measure of success, a decisive victory remained elusive; they were never able to either completely stop shipping traffic or to strike a blow such as they had on other communities. No buildings had been bombarded, no wharves or docks destroyed and their ability to conduct commerce remained fairly undamaged. Certainly, they had spread terror and kept quite fresh the general sense of fear that gripped all of New England, but this shadow victory was thus far all they'd been able to achieve. In fact, the situation had irritatingly led to two inadvertent improvements in favor of the Americans.

First, being unable to rely as heavily on maritime traffic to get goods into and out of port led to improvements in the road system, as a "wagon train" between Massachusetts and New York developed that allowed a steady stream of goods to continue to flow. Second, during the war, there were around 250 commissioned privateers holding contracts from the navy, and many operated out of New Bedford and Fairhaven in the battle-zone waters of the Northeast Atlantic seaboard. This force of mercenaries was efficient and well-motivated, capturing upward of 1,500 British prizes of all types during the conflict, most of which found themselves being auctioned off on the waterfronts of their would-be victims, making New Bedford/Fairhaven a sort of equivalent to Nova Scotia, where the English sent their captured prizes to be sold to the highest bidder and their crews interned (though in the United States, British prisoners were most often sent far inland or to the south if they weren't paroled).

As with Falmouth, there was a special grudge between the captains of these two vessels and the towns that remained thorns in their side. These feelings, however, weren't only on the side of the English officers who just couldn't seem to finish off their foes. The townspeople had a particular hatred of the *Nimrod*, not only for the depredations it visited upon the Americans but also because it represented a bitterly missed opportunity. In late 1812, when *Nimrod* first arrived in America under the command of Lieutenant George Hilton, it made a navigational error in the unfamiliar waters and grounded on the rocks off the shore of Sconticut Neck. Though there were two navy gunboats guarding New Bedford Harbor, they failed to react, making no move to destroy the enemy ship while it was most vulnerable. The trapped vessel was able to free itself, slipping off the rocks at high tide, and the chance to do mortal damage or capture it was lost. This infuriated many people, particularly in Fairhaven, where the populace was overwhelmingly in favor of the war, and they chaffed at the lost opportunity.

A thick pall of haze concealed the approach of the raiders as *Superb* and *Nimrod* anchored off Clark's Point in the predawn hours, loading the barges with heavily armed men. Their mission was a simple hit-and-run raid, and the target was the main concentration of docks in Fairhaven. They would slip into the harbor and, once landed, commence to set alight any and all ships, wharves and commercial interests they could before the town of a little less than two thousand inhabitants could muster the militia. It was a small raid but an effective type repeated over and over all along the coast of New England, and given their shortage of manpower, the British had become quite adept at it. *Superb* and *Nimrod* had to take caution, for the morning light would reveal their position and begin an immediate gun duel with Fort Phoenix. But the barges would be on their way back by then, and they could slip away before the Americans could return fire, being preoccupied with the blaze that would soon be raging nearby. But luck would not be with the British that morning.

Though the haze allowed the eight barges now rowing toward the city some cover, the tide and wind conditions had slowed the ships arrival and delayed their loading. Consequently, they were not in position to begin their approach until much closer to dawn than anticipated, and the sun was fast rising by the time they began to near the city. As members of the raiding party neared the Acushnet Bridge, to their surprise and horror, they heard a horn sound and the clatter of horses pierce the predawn air. Believing that their position had been given away and a detachment of dragoons was bearing down on them, the attack group, under the orders of Lieutenant James Garland, immediately turned to make for the safety of *Superb* and *Nimrod*. They could ill afford to have a running gun battle with a cavalry unit, who most always served as the vanguard for a larger body of infantry, and so they put their backs to their oars as fast as they could row. Before they could pass Palmer Island, they were spotted by the garrison at Fort Phoenix under the command of Lieutenant Selleck Osborne, who immediately began to fire several of the fort's dozen iron cannon, sending an unmistakable warning to the towns nearby.

A general alarm was raised on both sides of the harbor as women and children began to evacuate the towns for the safety of the surrounding countryside while the militia began to quickly arm and organize themselves for combat. Luckily for the British sailors, the barges were able to make it back to the ships as the odd shot splashed down nearby, though there were no actual hits from the militia before they were able to haul up their anchors and depart in haste. In a great twist of irony, they would not find

The volume of fire from Fort Phoenix was enough to deter any attacker and provided a stout defense that the British simply did not have the resources to overcome. *Courtesy Schlitzer90 (own work) [CC-BY-SA-3.0 (http://creativecommons.org/licenses/by-sa/3.0)], via Wikimedia Commons.*

out until much later, as the Americans laughed at them, that the horn they heard blowing that morning turned out to be a postman making his rounds. He sounded his tin horn to signal that he carried mail for the town, and the clatter of his single horse's hooves must have echoed to make it sound—in the imaginations of the jittery attackers—as if there were far more horses present.

Thus, both New Bedford and Fairhaven were spared the sting of battle on the back of a few fortuitously overactive imaginations and would not come under threat again during the war, this turning out to be the raiders' final visit to their waters. *Nimrod* and *Superb* set sail heading east, farther into the bay, and the militia interpreted this as a preemptive move on Mattapoisett. As they assembled, they began to march in that direction as men poured in from all over the area, and soon there were about six hundred militiamen in the town prepared to meet any further English aggression at the beach. It would be for naught, however, for as the militiamen made their camp in and around Mattapoisett, the raiders had already chosen a new target.

# HOPE THE WAR WOULD PASS IT BY

After the debacle at Fairhaven, the British determined to set their sights on a somewhat softer target with at least some small guarantee of success. Wareham had, to this point, hoped that the war would simply pass it by, as had the Revolutionary War (in which the town itself was spared the ignominy of destruction, though the brave citizens of the town sent their wood, iron and blood to the conflict when called on). This was not so much a naïve hope as it was a conception by the citizens of Wareham that, as previously discussed, they exhibited an appearance of neutrality, neither trumpeting loudly for war though certainly not shying from it if called on to defend their liberties. During the period after the Revolution up to the Civil War (and in some cases beyond), there existed in all states of the Union a substantial body of laws related to the raising, maintenance and mustering of militia companies for the common defense.

While Wareham was as loyally patriotic as any other municipality, it only minimally adhered to the laws regarding the number of men and amount of training required for the militia, with many people in the town believing that taking an openly martial stance invited trouble and precluded alternate avenues for resolving conflict. Many people in general, not just in Wareham, believed the militia system was in desperate need of reform, in any case. Based on the British system, militias were drawn from the body of adult male citizens of a community or local region. Because there were usually few regular army troops garrisoned in any one area, the militia served an important role in local conflicts, particularly when too few regular troops were available. Regulation of the militia was codified by the Continental Congress in the Articles of Confederation. The congress also created a full-time regular army—to be called by the now well-known name "the Continental Army"—but related to chronic manpower shortages and growing pains in the new country, the militia provided short-term support to the regulars throughout the Revolution.

# MILITIA SERVICE

During colonial times, militia service was distinguished from military service in that service in the regular army was normally for a fixed period of time (usually at least one year) for a specified salary, whereas militia was only expected to meet a specific threat, or to prepare to meet a threat, for a short period of time, most often defined by the duration of the emergency. Militiamen usually provided their own weapons, equipment or supplies. Officers and NCOs were elected and, if they had the funds, might wear a uniform to distinguish them from the enlisted men, although they could be compensated for losses or were sometimes provided with equipment not normally owned by private citizens, such as artillery pieces, which were considered "public property." Based on many of these qualities, militia were also considered far less organized and poorly trained, though, like the people who made up the service, their quality varied from unit to unit.

The general unpopularity of the militia was well summed up by George C. Beckwith well after the war but reflects a sentiment not uncommon long before his words were spoken on behalf of the American Peace Society: "The demoralizing influences even of our own militia drills has long been notorious to a proverb. It has been a source of general corruptions to the community, and formed habits of idleness, dissipation and profligacy...musterfields have generally been scenes or occasions of gambling, licentiousness, and almost every vice...An eye-witness of a New England training, so late as 1845, says, 'beastly drunkenness, and other immoralities, were enough to make good men shudder at the very name of a muster.'" Martial stances and peaceful resolution aside, however, the plain fact that faced Wareham when the war of 1812 came to its doorstep was that it was unprepared for the conflict.

## SAVAGE BETRAYAL

Though the sun was not yet quite up, the morning of June 13, 1814, promised to be a clear and sunny day. *Nimrod* had for the past two years been a regular and fearful sight in the bay, but given the razor-thin margin by which Fairhaven and New Bedford had escaped its assault with the intent to raze their communities to the ground the day before, the citizens of the forty or so dwellings in the small hamlet of Mattapoisett were filled with particular dread when the ship appeared just outside of the cove.

The English navy had bottled up New England, burning its ships and keeping its inhabitants in a constant state of fear for two solid years, a fact to which many had become inured, but only recently had the navy torn away any pretense of decency in wartime and begun the wholesale indiscriminant destruction of all property—public and private—with little regard for any life that got in the way of its machinations. Militia had been pouring into the area all night and continued to arrive with messages of what had transpired while preparing to meet the enemy on the shores they were sure the British were about to land on at any moment. Convinced of the intentions of the raider to wreak havoc, the inhabitants of the town did all they could to avoid its depredations. They hurriedly buried their valuables and prepared to move to the nearby woods as the ship passed menacingly by.

The ship did not stop, however, passing out of sight as it slipped by Pine Island, and the townspeople breathed a collective sigh of relief. They were safe, even if only for the moment. Ebenezer Bourne, a resident of nearby Wareham who was in the area at the time, recognized that if the ship kept on its current northeasterly course, however, there was a good possibility that it might be doing what to this point had been unthinkable: heading into the shallow waters and making for the head of Buzzards Bay. Bourne continued to shadow the ship along the shore as it slowly made its way through the quiet sea. By around 11:30 a.m., the *Nimrod* had set its anchor just south of Bird Island, and Bourne, recognizing the danger immediately, set about to secure a small boat so that he might get word to the town before it was too late.

Bourne arrived in Wareham shortly after noon to raise an alarm, for though he had seen *Nimrod* begin to make its way south back toward its base at Tarpaulin Cove, he was convinced of its intention to return. Word began to spread almost electrically, and a messenger was soon dispatched to nearby Agawam, where Captain Israel Fearing Jr., commander of the local militia, lived. No one had as of yet called for a muster of troops, and Agawam was some three miles away from the docks and on the other side of the river from Fearing, so he began to make as much haste as possible to prepare himself and begin gathering men.

Meanwhile, Bourne's intuition was to be proven correct as the residents of Great Neck spied six barges loaded with about two hundred men making their way toward the entrance of the Weweantic River, not far beyond which lay the docks of Wareham. Even though they were still some distance off, it could clearly be seen that the men were heavily armed, their pikes and bayonets glinting in the late-day sun. The citizens of the town had not seen the raiders coming in, however, until they were fairly close to the town, almost in Mark's Cove, their approach having been masked by the prominence of Great Hill to the southwest and aided greatly by the speed their sails and oars afforded them, gliding almost silently toward their target.

Fluttering from a spit on the bow of the lead barge was a small white flag of truce, a dubious indication that the British were not there to attack the town but simply to speak with its inhabitants. There were those who still held out hope that this was true, and no one wished to make a hasty move if they could somehow escape battle. There were many who were filled with anger at the British for all the suffering they'd endured and wished to fire on them as soon as they were within range, but there were also cooler heads who opined that the speed with which the invaders were coming precluded the townspeople's ability to evacuate their families to safety before their foes arrived. Better to speak with and possibly appease them than to risk harm to their loved ones, who were only a short distance away.

## LANDING

A scant hour later, the barges landed at Leonard's Wharf, and the sailors began to quickly disembark. They were met by a small delegation of community leaders, who had elected William Fearing, Esq., to speak for them, gingerly carrying their own flag of truce: a handkerchief tied to the handle of a cane. They approached as Lieutenant Garland, once again in command of the ship's landing parties, stepped onto the dock and requested a parlay with him. Garland stated that he was there to seize and destroy some ships from Plymouth and any ships or property belonging to Falmouth as well. He then demanded the citizens immediately identify all Wareham public property, stating it would not be harmed so long as they cooperated with him and made no move to hinder his operations.

This last point proved to be mere deception, for Captain Newton had sent the landing parties to Wareham with the express orders that they make for the town's cotton mill and salt works with all haste and burn them to the ground. To accomplish this, he had sent three of his barges upstream to land closer to the mill while the other three occupied the townspeople near the wharf. Garland required that the Americans agree not to harass or in any way attack his men and made certain that they understood that were there any violation of this agreement, *Nimrod* would be called to come in and bombard the town with the intention of destroying all buildings within range of its guns. The delegation agreed to the terms and readily pointed out the ships belonging to Falmouth, at which point the main body of enemy troops marched to the shipyard belonging to Roland Leonard, Esq., a prosperous businessman (and a veteran of the Revolution), with firebrands at the ready.

Meanwhile, three barges landed at the Wareham Narrows, and sparks were seen to be flying from the lead barge. Seconds later, there was a sharp hiss as the crew launched a Congreve rocket, which streaked away on a red trail and flew true to its target, plunging into the first floor of the cotton mill and setting it alight. Several townspeople rushed to fight the rapidly growing fire over the shouted threats of the sailors who promised to put anyone who attempted to save the factory to the sword. At the shipyard, the sailors immediately set fire to four schooners belonging to Falmouth and a fifth ship belonging to Plymouth. As the burning vessels began to dip beneath the water, the flag of truce came down and the sailors continued into the shipyard, their intent to burn any ships to be found therein, regardless of ownership, apparent.

The townspeople cursed Garland for his deception, protesting the destruction of their property and accusing him of taking advantage of them under false promises. The lieutenant now required some better form of protection, as the townspeople began to call out that the militia should assemble. The marines seized about a dozen citizens, many of them children and some men, among them Dr. Mackie, the town's physician, and brought them to the barges moored nearby, threatening them with death if anyone made a move to attack the sailors or to interfere with their handiwork.

By this time, Captain Fearing had arrived and in his haste had only been able to assemble and arm ten men, who ran without hesitation to the beach to meet the enemy. The enemy's possession of hostages, however, made for a tense situation. An account printed in the September 6, 1834 issue of the *Norfolk Advertiser* written twenty years after the event gives eyewitness details to the event:

> *The position of the barges was favorable for capture, being left in charge of only four guards, and not more than 30 yards opposite the little point of land upon which the brave Fearing and his associates appeared. Rushing from the woods, burning with the ardor of patriotism, and stimulated with a wish for revenge, they came wholly unexpected upon the guard; a firm but Spartan band. The sentry quailed as they drew to their shoulders their unerring war weapons, and but for the hostages which the wily enemy had placed in their boats, they would have tasted death, their barges been scuttled and their means to escape wholly destroyed.*

# Charge

The order was given to "Charge!" and the little phalanx—swelling with enthusiasm that no language can describe, and with determined bravery that nothing can withstand—feeling themselves an army, marched with firm and solemn steps to the beach and, to be sure of their mark, to their waists in water and in the silence raised their muskets to face, ready to receive the fatal order. The gallant captain, knowing no love in this instance but that of his country, with a stentorian voice gave the order to "Aim!" This was a case of life or death for the physician. "Fire!" was to follow. The last word was breaking on the lips of the infuriated commander when the hostage, in a voice of despair, cried, "For God's sake, don't fire!"

"I will!" shouted the brave Israel.

"Don't you know me?" again cried the hostage.

"No," returned the Patriot in a still louder voice.

"I'm your doctor!"

"I don't know you!" said the hero.

"I'm your friend"

"I don't know you!" said the captain again.

"Fire men!" reiterated the impatient captain in a voice of thunder, no longer able to suppress his feelings while his country and his friend were both before him.

He knew which to choose. The men, however, with deep compassion for their friend and physician, a man whom they all loved and respected and, being less zealous of their rights, resolved not to fire. They recovered their arms and drew back on the beach. This resolution saved the life of the hostage.

William Fearing made his own protest against the destruction of the town's private property when Garland and a band of sailors stopped in his store and began to help themselves to some of his liquor. He tried in vain to convince them that he was their friend and that the townspeople had done nothing to provoke them again and again, but Garland simply dismissed his pleas saying that if he was their friend, then he was an enemy to his country.

# Ships Ablaze

The sailors then walked from the lawyer's store and, drunk on his liquor, set fire to his boat moored nearby. The shipyard was in blazes, with the sloops

A depiction of the landing of HMS *Nimrod* troops in Wareham in June 1814. *Illustration by Josephine Thoms, photo courtesy of Cailtin Flaherty.*

*William Lucy, Thomas, Experiment, Paragon* and *William* burning. Joining them were the schooners *Fancy, Industry, Elizabeth, Nancy* and *Argus,* as well as the brigs *William Richmond* and *Independent.* In all, twelve ships would feel the burn of the torch, damaging almost three thousand total tons of shipping in one swoop. The cotton mill escaped total destruction, having been rescued by a brave and determined band of townspeople, though in the chaos, their salt works had also been set alight, and they had been unable to save it, being unable to approach the area, lest they come under the fire of the sailors' muskets.

Lieutenant Garland decided that his objectives had been met, particularly considering that the people were becoming restive and militia were beginning to appear in greater numbers. The sailors would soon be too far outnumbered and outgunned for the hostages to provide any protection, so Garland had them loaded in pairs in the barges and raised his flag of truce once more. As they began to make their way down the narrow river, first one shot and then another rang out from the shore. Having just arrived on the scene, many militiamen didn't realize that the British raiders were carrying hostages and, cursing the inaction of the people on the scene for cowardice, began to take shots at the barges. Fortunately, Captain Fearing was informed of the situation, and he quickly ordered a stop to the ragged volleys when he learned there were hostages aboard.

It must have been a tense milieu for the prisoners in those few moments, wondering if they would get a bullet from their enemies or their friends, as musket balls whizzed over their heads. Garland sailed to the far end of Cromeset Neck, where he ordered the hostages put ashore, and then as his barges turned out to the bay, each fired a Congreve rocket and their swivel gun in the direction of Wareham, though they were too far out of range for them to actually hit anything. These were little more than desultory parting shots. The crews all gave three cheers as they rowed away and returned to their ships by late afternoon, leaving Wareham smoldering in their wake.

Though differing accounts give various estimates of the monetary damage done, many agree that the damage to the mill, town and ships came to around $20,000 and the salt works at $500,000. In current values, that would be roughly $350,000 and $6.5 million, respectively, a tidy sum in 1812 and certainly still one today. For the British, it had been a small but successful raid, with Captain Paget reporting the conduct of his men as "exemplary" and saying that "despite the temptations of liquor, etc.... [they] strictly [held] sacred private property." The Americans saw it a bit differently, describing it as "a damned shame and disgrace to any nation to come in under a flag of truce and commit the greatest outrage possible, then return under a flag of truce." Still, there was more shame to go around. Six days after the attack, on June 20, 1814, two young men were arrested for treason for assisting the British in the attempt to enter the harbor and the attack on Wareham.

They were committed for trial in the circuit court in Boston but were eventually found innocent and released. News of the attack on Wareham spread quickly and sensationally, and by the next day, the town was a veritable fortress. No other forces made an attempt to molest the town during the war, and by the time *Nimrod* had set sail again, to anyone attempting such an endeavor, the entire south coast of Massachusetts would have seemed a hornet's nest.

*Chapter 9*

# THE END OF THE HUNTER

*And still the earth's no happier*
*Than in the silent days*
*When men were content with simple joys*
*And restful quiet ways*
—*Joseph Dorr,* Babylon, a Historical Romance in Rhyme of the Time
of Nimrod, the Mighty Hunter King, *1897*

H MS *Nimrod* continued to raid off Rhode Island that summer. The ship,
named after the great hunter Nimrod, of the Old Testament, had
been commissioned to seek out and destroy American privateers so hated
by the British. During the course of its engagement in New England, during
the War of 1812, the *Nimrod* struck fear into the heart of New Englanders
up and down the coast.

The HMS *Nimrod,* a brig, often called a "sloop-of-war," was a small ship with
a single gun deck that carried between ten and eighteen cannons. Nathaniel
Mitchell was the first captain of the *Nimrod* in 1812. The *Nimrod* arrived
along the New England coast sometime in the fall of 1813 and the threat of
it and other British ships prowling the was enough strike fear in the hearts of
those living in the towns bordering Buzzards and Narragansett Bays, Block

Island and Nantucket Sound. The *Nimrod* patrolled the New England coast as part of a fleet of British ships commanded by Commander Paget of the HMS *Superb*. It also included the HMS *Recruit* and the captured American ship the *Retaliation*. The fleet began preying on American privateers early in October of 1813 along Cape Cod.

## TERROR OF THE FISHERMEN

The British blockade of New England was particularly devastating on the region's fishing industry. According to Leonard Bolles Ellis in *History of New Bedford and Its Vicinity, 1602–1892*: "The *Nimrod* was a great annoyance to the fishermen along the coast, who were frequently captured and set free after their catch of fresh fish had been transferred to the larder of the brig. Records show instances where hundreds of pounds were taken; and so it happened that every body stood in constant fear of losing his catch."

## CONFUSING HISTORY

There is a confused history concerning the HMS *Nimrod* and its grounding in Buzzards Bay in 1814. The most popular story is that the day after the June 13, 1814 attack on Wareham, the *Nimrod* sailed south into Buzzards Bay and got stuck on a ledge along Quick's Hole, a narrow strait between Buzzards Bay and the Vineyard Sound. It is located due north of Menemsha, a small fishing village located in the town of Chilmark on the island of Martha's Vineyard, and due south of New Bedford. It extends about one and a half miles from north to south and is three-quarters of a mile across at its widest point.

According to the story, the high tide was not sufficient to free the ship, so the Captain Vincent Newton made the decision to jettison several of the cannon to lighten the load. Sufficiently lightened, the ship was able to set itself free and sail away. Unfortunately, this story appears to be a combination of two separate incidents.

# RUNNING AGROUND

After its attack on Wareham on June 13, 1814, the *Nimrod* reportedly sailed south through Buzzards Bay heading toward Cape Cod. In order to get there, the ship had to pass through the shallows at Quick's Hole. This should not have been not a problem since it had passed through there many times; in fact, the *Nimrod* had just sailed through the narrow strait the day before to get to Wareham.

According to reports, at 6:00 a.m., the *Nimrod* weighed anchor at the head of Buzzards Bay, put out its sails and set a course south, and by 11:30 a.m., it headed into Quick's Hole. Unfortunately, the tide was low and the captain had overestimated the depth of the water on the ship's starboard side. The *Nimrod* struck the shore. The captain of the vessel ordered that the sails be taken in to keep the ship from being driven farther onto shore. Because the bow of the ship and its starboard side were stuck, an anchor was dropped from the stern. If the anchor stuck fast, the ship could be hauled backward off the shore by hauling the anchor in. Grounding on the shore was not considered the worst thing that could happen to the *Nimrod* and although an inconvenience, it was thought to be easily resolved. It wasn't, however, at least not immediately. Stuck on the ledge, the *Nimrod* would be easy prey for attack by American ships. Luckily, the *Superb* was nearby to chase off any would-be attackers.

The stern anchor was not working to free the stuck vessel, but it had at least stopped the ship from drifting any farther into shore. After consulting with Commander Paget on board the *Superb*, it was decided that if the *Nimrod* lightened its load, it could free itself from the ledge. It was decided to unload some of the ship's cannons to lighten the load on board, free the ship and then reload the cannons after the *Nimrod* was free. Crew members did not want to leave behind any artillery that the American forces could salvage and ultimately use against them. The cannons were taken from the starboard side of the ship, and when the tide rose, the *Nimrod* was able to free itself. Reportedly, the cannons were reloaded back onto the ship, and the *Nimrod* and *Superb* set course for Gay Head on Martha's Vineyard.

Captain Newton's log described the event:

> *14th June At 6 Weighed* [anchor]– *running towards Quick's Hole. At 11:30 hawled up for the Hole. At 12:30 observed the Brig* [Nimrod] *to strike the shore. Shortened and furled the sails. Employed getting anchor out astern to Heave her off. Boat from Superb came to our assistance. Got out several of the Guns and Shot. At 3:30 Hove her off & anchored with the Small Bower. At 6 Weighed and stood towards the Superb. At 7:30 anchored off Gay Head.*

## ANOTHER VERSION OF THE GROUNDING

The second incident regarding the grounding of the *Nimrod* also reportedly took place in 1814 following the attack on Wareham. According to reports, the *Nimrod* was in hot pursuit of the American ship *Harmony* in Buzzards Bay. The *Harmony* was able to trick the Nimrod into running aground off Round Hill in Dartmouth.

According to Craig S. Chartier of the Plymouth Archaeological Rediscovery Project in his report, "*Nimrod* or Not: A Report on the Cannons Recovered in 1998 by the Kendall Whaling Museum," when the *Harmony* reached New Bedford Harbor, its sails were full of holes. According to Chartier, "*Harmony* was said to have been off loaded in a snowstorm, indicating this story may have happened in the winter. George Taber reported in the late nineteenth century that his father related to him that when *Nimrod* went aground he rode down Sconticut Neck and found a number of people gathered on the shore watching the stranded *Nimrod*. The ship then came off safely at high tide."

Chartier reported that these two incidents "appear to have been combined to create the notion that the *Nimrod* went aground off Round Hill on June 14, 1814 and had to lighten her load by dumping some of her cannons and shot. Some may try to make the case that the two incidents were one and the same, that the *Nimrod* ran aground on June 14 after attacking Wareham and while chasing the *Harmony*. Unfortunately, the two incidents appear to be separate and unique for several reasons the most foremost being that after the attack on Wareham, *Nimrod* sailed south towards Quick's Hole while during the *Harmony* chase she sailed north towards New Bedford."

Further evidence points to Newton's own logbook, in which he recorded the grounding at Quick's Hole, not the case after the *Harmony*.

## VARIOUS ACCOUNTS

There were various accounts given about the incidents involving the grounding of the *Nimrod*. As Ellis describes in *History of New Bedford and Its Vicinity, 1602–1892*:

> *George H. Taber relates that his father rode hastily down Sconticut Neck, and found a number of people gathered on the shore, who were watching the stranded vessel and endeavoring to organize an expedition to attack her.*

*The* Nimrod *came off safely at high tide, however, before the plans were completed. Capt. Russell Maxfield remembers the event, and the expressions of indignation against the gunboats. Their final departure from the port created no serious apprehensions of danger.*

Ellis goes on to recount Thomas Durfee's account of the event:

*"I saw the* Harmony,*" said Thomas Durfee, "when she sailed up to Rotch's wharf, and her sails were perforated with cannon shot. She was taken above the bridge and moored in the stream. Among the articles in her cargo was a lot of skins, which were taken to Boston in the sloop* Boston, *Capt. Philip Mosher; and I remember that when she cleared it was in a driving snow storm."*

## CANNONS FOUND

Accordingly, this incident led investigators in the 1980s to identify the site of the grounding as being off Round Hill in Dartmouth. For years, the debate raged on as to whether the *Nimrod* ran aground off Quick's Hole and dumped its cannons or whether the ship ran aground off Round Hill in Dartmouth and unloaded its cannons there.

In 1996, the Kendall Whaling Museum was sure that the *Nimrod* had grounded off Round Hill and began an underwater search. The search turned up three cannons. At the time, the cannons were hailed as remnants. The cannons that were found by the late Henry W. Kendall and David W. Schloerb were part of the Kendall Whaling Museum's collection until that institution merged with the New Bedford Whaling Museum. Three of the cannon were awarded to towns impacted by the *Nimrod*. Falmouth and Wareham each got one, stored in an alkaline bath of fresh water and sodium carbonate to reverse the ionization of the iron and stabilize the metal for later display.

All the cannons that were recovered measure fifty-four inches long, and the bore of the Wareham example is just under three inches. They are the same measurements for three-pounder cannons used in the late eighteenth century.

During the course of researching the cannons that are now held by various historical societies in southern New England, it was discovered that the cannons likely did not come from the *Nimrod* at all but that they represent an even more important find: potentially the remains of a Revolutionary

The Falmouth cannons were found and had suffered the impact of the time. Despite the fact that cannons were found, their connection to the *Nimrod* could not be verified. *Courtesy of Falmouth Historical Society.*

War ship, either a British or an American vessel.

Only the Wareham cannon and the carronade in the possession of the New Bedford Whaling Museum have any visible markings. The Wareham cannon has a "6" stamped on the barrel. This number is a founder's (iron works manufacturer) mark indicating the weight of the cannon itself. The six means that the cannon weighed six hundred-weight, a one hundred-weight being 112 pounds. The New Bedford Whaling Museum carronade has the date 1778 stamped on it, the date of manufacture, corresponding to its earliest production. The types of cannon recovered all appear to be three- or (less likely) four-pounders. Whether or not the cannons came from the *Nimrod*, they remain treasures of Buzzards Bay and a remembrance of the War of 1812 and its impact on Wareham and other New England towns along the coast.

## THE *NIMROD* WRECKED

The HMS *Nimrod*, the great hunter, was wrecked on a rock off the coast of Wales in 1827, salvaged and sold out of naval service. It was reported that on January 14, 1827, when on its way from Cork to the river Clyde, the HMS *Nimrod* was sheltered in Whole Wheat Bay during a gale, but the storm drove the ship ashore and it bilged.

"Bilged" refers to the deliberate or accidental flooding of the bilge, the lowest compartment of a ship, below the waterline. This incapacitates the

The *Nimrod* reportedly either dumped its cannons at Quick's Hole in Buzzards Bay or off Round Hill in Dartmouth. *Courtesy of Falmouth Historical Society.*

ship. When done accidentally by grounding, it usually results in the ship being entirely lost. Help came for the grounded *Nimrod*, but by the time it arrived, the *Nimrod* had managed to free itself. However, the damage to the ship was too severe, and the vessel was sold.

In 1840, New Bedford merchant seaman George Tabor reported that when he was a mate on the ship *Samuel Robertson*, he saw *Nimrod* taking on cargo in Mobile Bay, appearing no longer as the great hunter and terror of the New England coast.

And so the scourge of New England, the HMS *Nimrod*, finally met its match—time and the sea—a formidable match for anyone. And although long gone, the memory of its attack on Wareham in June 1814 remains as an inimical part of the history and collective reminiscence of the inhabitants of Wareham today.

*Appendix I*

# NIMROD TIMELINE

January 27, 1814: appears at Tarpaulin Cove

January 29, 1814: bombed Falmouth

April 5, 1814: captured the *Sally Hallett*

June 5, 1814: ordered Swedish brig *Carolus Magnus* back to New Bedford

June 6, 1814: captured pilot boat *Number 1* in Buzzards Bay

June 9, 1814: captured sloop *Polly* off Westport

June 13, 1814: attempted to land at New Bedford

June 14, 1814: sited off Bird Island in Mattapoisett

June 14, 1814: attacked Wareham

June 14, 1814: grounded off Quick's Hole

June 14, 1814: anchored off Gay Head

August 5, 1814: captured sloop *Eagle* off Point Judith, Rhode Island

August 6, 1814: five boats taken off Watch Hill

August 9, 1814: attacked Stonington

September 10, 1814: captured four New Bedford boats from Point Judith

January 14, 1827: grounded off Wales and sold

*Appendix II*

# LETTER FROM
# WAREHAM, 1814

*To the editor of the* New Bedford Mercury:

Sirs—Yesterday morning we were informed of the approach of the enemy and at about 11 o' clock A.M. they landed at the village called the Narrows with a flag. There were six barges containing two hundred and twenty men. They demanded (before the proper authority could arrive) all the public property; and declared, that in case they were molested, every house within their reach should be consumed. We were not prepared to make any opposition and promised not to. To prevent a violation on our part, they detained a number of men and boys as prisoners for their security; declaring that if any of their men were injured they [American prisoners] should be put to immediate death. Having stationed sentries back of the village, they proceeded to fire the vessels and cotton manufactory. Twelve vessels were fired, five of which were totally destroyed; the remainder were extinguished after the enemy departed. The cotton manufactory was also extinguished. Damage estimated at 20,000 dollars. It is supposed that the enemy came from the *Nimrod* brig and *Superb 74*.
BENJA. BOURNE
BENJA. FEARING
Selectmen of Wareham
—Reprinted by Hesekiah Niles and William Ogden Niles, *Niles' Weekly Register* 6 (1814).

# BIBLIOGRAPHY

Adams, James Truslow. *The Founding of New England.* Boston: Atlantic-Little, Brown, 1921.

Albion, Robert G., William A. Baker and Benjamin Labaree. *New England and the Sea.* Mystic, CT: Wesleyan University Press, 1972.

Allen, Joseph. *Battles of the British Navy from A.D. 1000 to 1840.* Vol. 2. Charleston, SC: Nabu Press, 2011.

Allison, Robert J. *A Short History of Cape Cod.* Beverly, MA: Commonwealth Editions, 2010.

Ashley, Clifford Warren. *The Yankee Whaler.* Mineloa, NY: Courier Dover Publications, 1942.

Bangs, Mary Rogers. *Old Cape Cod: The Land, the Men, the Sea.* Boston: Houghton Mifflin Co., 1920.

Banvard, Joseph. *Plymouth and the Pilgrims; or, Incidents of Adventure in the History of the First Settlers.* Charleston, SC: Gould and Lincoln, 1851.

Batchelder, Samuel. "Some Sea Terms in Land Speech." *New England Quarterly* (1929).

Barto, Jean, and Doris Mackenzie. *Humor, Heartache & Harrowing Tales Keeping Memories Alive.* Bloomington, IN: Trafford Publishing, 2006.

Beale, Thomas. *The Natural History of the Sperm Whale.* London, England: Little Hampton, 1839.

Bidwell, Percy. "The Agricultural Revolution in New England." *American Historical Review* (1921).

Bourne, Silvanus. *The Plymouth County Directory and Historical Register of the Old Colony*. Middleboro, MA: Stillman B. Pratt & Co., 1867.

Brown, Alice. "Cape Cod Cranberries." In *New England: The Companion Library*. Boston, MA: Perry Mason Co., 1898.

Burgess, Ebenezer. *Wareham—Sixty Years Since: A Discourse Delivered at Wareham, Massachusetts*. Middleboro, MA: T.R. Marvin & Son, 1861.

Burrows, Frederika. *Cannonballs & Cranberries*. Middleboro, MA: William S. Sullwold, 1976.

Bushnell, David. "The Treatment of the Indians in Plymouth Colony." *New England Quarterly* (June 1953).

Carstens, Patrick Richard. *Searching for the Forgotten War—1812: United States of America*. Bloomington, IN: Xlibris Corporation, 2011.

Church, Albert Cook. *Whale Ships and Whaling*. New York: W.W. Norton & Company, 1938.

Clark, A. Howard. "The American Whale Fishery." *Science* (April 1887) (American Association for the Advancement of Science).

Clark, Charles E., James S. Leamon and Karen Bowden. *Maine in the Early Republic: From Revolution to Statehood*. Lebanon, NH: University Press of New England, 1988.

Clowes, William Laird, and H.W. Wilson. *The Royal Navy: A History from the Earliest Times to 1900*. Rochester Kent, England: Chatham Publishing, 1996.

Collins, Gilbert. *Guidebook to the Historic Sites of the War of 1812*. Toronto, Ontario: Dundurn, 2006.

Cook, John A. *Pursuing the Whale*. Boston, MA: Houghton Mifflin Company, 1926.

Cox, Robert, and Jacob Walker. *Massachusetts Cranberry Culture: A History from Bog to Table*. Charleston, SC: The History Press, 2012.

De Kay, James. *The Battle of Stonington: Torpedoes, Submarines, and Rockets in the War of 1812*. Annapolis, MD: Naval Institute Press, 2013.

Deyo, Simeon. *History of Barnstable County, Massachusetts, 1620–1890*. Boston, MA: W. Blake & Co., 1890.

Dudley, Paul. "An Essay upon the Natural History of Whales, with a Particular Account of the Ambergris Found in the Sperma Ceti Whale, 1724–1725." *Philosophical Transactions of the Royal Society*, 1996.

Ellis, James. *A Ruinous and Unhappy War: New England and the War of 1812*. New York: Algora Publishing, 2009.

Ellis, Leonard Bolles. *History of New Bedford and Its Vicinity, 1602–1892*. Syracuse, NY: Mason Publishing, 1892.

Elting, John. *Amateurs to Arms: A Military History of the War of 1812*. Chapel Hill, NC: Algonquin Books, 1991.

Feintuch, Burt, and David Watters. *The Encyclopedia of New England.* New Haven, CT: Yale University Press, 2005.

Field, Edward. *State of Rhode Island and Providence Plantations at the End of the Century: A History.* Syracuse, NY: Mason Publishing, 1902.

Fitz-Enz, David, and David G. Fitz-Enz. *Hacks, Sycophants, Adventurers, and Heroes: Madison's Commanders in the War of 1812.* Lanham, MD: Taylor Trade Publications, 2012.

Fredriksen, John. *War of 1812 Eyewitness Accounts: An Annotated Bibliography.* Westport, CT: Greenwood Press, 1997.

Freeman, Frederick. *The History of Cape Cod: The Annals of Barnstable County and of Its Several Towns, Including the District of Mashpee.* Boston: Parnassus Imprints, 1865.

Hannings, Bud. *The War of 1812: A Complete Chronology with Biographies of 63 General Officers.* Jefferson, NC: McFarland, 2012.

Heidler, David Stephen, and Jeanne T. Heidler. *Encyclopedia of the War of 1812.* Annapolis, MD: Naval Institute Press, 2004.

Hickey, Donald. *The War of 1812: A Forgotten Conflict.* Champaign: University of Illinois Press, 1989.

———. *The War of 1812: A Short History.* Champaign: University of Illinois Press, 1995.

Hurd, D. Hamilton. *History of Plymouth County, Massachusetts with Biographical Sketches of Many of the Pioneers and Prominent Men.* Boston: J.W. Lewis and Co., 1884.

James, William. *Naval Occurrences of the War of 1812: A Full and Correct Account of the Naval War Between Great Britain and the United States of America, 1812–1815.* Annapolis, MD: Naval Institute Press, 2004.

Kelley, Shawnie M. *It Happened on Cape Cod.* Guilford, CT: TwoDot (1st ed.), 2006.

Kittredge, Henry C. *Cape Cod: Its People and Their History.* Boston: Houghton Mifflin Co., 1930.

Kurlansky, Mark. *Cod: A Biography of the Fish That Changed the World.* New York: Random House, 2011.

Latimer, Jon. *1812: War with America.* Cambridge, MA: Harvard University Press, 2007.

Lavery, Brian. *The Arming and Fitting of English Ships of War, 1600–1815.* London, England: Conway Maritime Press, 1987.

Leighton, Clare. *Where Land Meets Sea: The Enduring Cape Cod.* Boston: David R. Godine, 1954.

Little, Frances. *Early American Textiles.* New York: Century Co., 1931.

Lombard, Percival Hall. *The Aptuxet Trading Post: The First Trading Post of the Plymouth Colony, with an Account of Its Restoration on the Original Foundations.* Bourne, MA: Bourne Historical Society, 1934.

Lossing, Benson John. *The Pictorial Field-book of the War of 1812; or, Illustrations, by Pen and Pencil, of the History, Biography, Scenery, Relics, and Traditions of the Last War for American Independence.* New York: Harper & Brothers, 1868.

Lyons, David. *The Sailing Navy List: All the Ships of the Royal Navy, Built, Purchased and Captured, 1688–1860.* London, England: Conway Maritime Press, 1993.

Mahon, John K. *The War of 1812.* New York: DaCapo Press, 1991.

Maine Historical Society. *Collections and Proceedings of the Maine Historical Society.* Vol. 5. Bangor, ME: Brown Thurston Co., 1894.

McCusker, John J., and Russell R. Menard. *The Economy of British America, 1607–1789.* Chapel Hill: University of North Carolina Press, 1985.

Mitchell, F. "Cape Cod." *Century Magazine*, September 1883.

Morison, Samuel Eliot. *Maritime History of Massachusetts, 1783–1860.* Boston: Houghton Mifflin Co., 1921.

Murdoch, Richard. "The Battle of Orleans, Massachusetts (1814) and Associated Events." *American Neptune* 24 (1964).

Nason, Elias. *A Gazetteer of the State of Massachusetts with Numerous Illustrations.* Boston: B.B. Russell, 1890.

*[The] New England Gazetteer*, 1839: John Hayward-Boyd & White.

Niles, Hezekiah, and William Ogden Niles. *Niles' Weekly Register* 6 (1814).

Nordhoff, Charles. "Cape Cod, Nantucket, and the Vineyard." *Harper's New Monthly Magazine* LI (1875).

Perkins, Edwin J. *The Economy of Colonial America.* New York: Columbia University Press, 1988.

Pizzolato, Susan, and Lynda Ames Byrne. *Wareham.* Mount Pleasant, SC: Arcadia Publishing, 2002.

Powell, Lydia. *Historic Towns of New England.* Albany, NY: Knickerbocker Press, 1898.

Prude, Jonathan. *The Coming of Industrial Order: Town and Factory Life in Rural Massachusetts, 1810–1860.* Amherst: University of Massachusetts Press, 1983.

Quinn, William P. *The Saltworks of Historic Cape Cod: A Record of the Nineteenth-Century Economic Boom in Barnstable County.* Marstons Mills, MA: Parnassus Imprints, 1993.

Rider, Raymond A. *Life and Times in Wareham over 200 Years, 1739–1939.* Middleboro, MA: Wareham Historical Society, 1989.

Ridley, Scott. *Morning of Fire: John Kendrick's Daring American Odyssey in the Pacific.* New York: William Morrow, 2010.

Root-Bliss, William. *Colonial Days on Buzzards Bay*. Boston: Houghton, Mifflin and Co., 1888.

Rutland, Robert Allen. *The Presidency of James Madison*. Lawrence: University Press of Kansas, 1990.

Sears, Robert. "From the Briny Deep: Cannons Recovered from 1812 British Ship." *Patriot Ledger*, October 29, 1999.

Shepherd, James F., and Gary M. Walton. *Shipping, Maritime Trade, and the Economic Development of Colonial North America*. Cambridge, England: Cambridge University Press, 1972.

Skeen, Carl Edward. *Citizen Soldiers in the War of 1812*. Lexington: University Press of Kentucky, 1999.

Tunis, Edwin. *Colonial Craftsmen and the Beginnings of American Industry*. New York: World Publishing, 1965.

Turner, W. *British Generals in the War of 1812: High Command in the Canadas*. Kingston, Ontario: McGill-Queen's Press, 1999.

Vickers, Daniel. *Farmers and Fishermen: Two Centuries of Work in Essex County, Massachusetts, 1630–1850*. Chapel Hill: University of North Carolina Press, 1994.

Vuilleumier, Marion Rawson. *The Way It Was on Olde Cape Cod: The History, Personality and Way of Life of Early Settlers, Earning a Living on Olde Cape Cod*. Burlington, MA: Butterworth, 1968.

Webb, James. *Cape Cod Cranberries*. Carlisle, MA: Applewood Books, 2009.

Weston, Thomas. *History of the Town of Middleboro, Massachusetts*. Boston: Houghton, Mifflin, 1906.

Wheeler, Richard Anson. *History of the Town of Stonington, County of New London, Connecticut: From Its First Settlement in 1649 to 1900*. Stonington, CT: Press of the Day Publishing Company, 1900.

Winfield, Rif. *British Warships in the Age of Sail, 1793–1817: Design, Construction, Careers and Fates*. Barnsley, England: Seaforth Publishing, 2008.

Yonge, Charles Duke. *The History of the British Navy: From the Earliest Period to the Present Time*. London, England: R. Bentley, 1866.

Young, Alexander. *Chronicles of the First Planters of Massachusetts Bay, from 1623 to 1636*. Boston: Charles C. Little and James Brown, 1846.

# INDEX

# ABOUT THE AUTHORS

J. NORTH CONWAY is the author of a dozen nonfiction books, including *The Cape Cod Canal: Breaking Through the Bared and Bended Arm*, published by The History Press in 2008. He teaches at the University of Massachusetts–Dartmouth and Bridgewater State University.

JESSE DUBUC was born and raised in southeastern Massachusetts and developed his love of history by being raised on the soil soaked in it. *Attack of the HMS Nimrod* is his first nonfiction work.

*Visit us at*
www.historypress.net
..................................................................
*This title is also available as an e-book*